PASTA LIGHT

PASTA LIGHT

GREAT-TASTING NO-FAT AND LOW-FAT RECIPES FOR HEALTHY EATING

Anne Sheasby

southwater

This edition is published by Southwater, an imprint of Anness Publishing Ltd,
Hermes House, 88–89 Blackfriars Road, London SE1 8HA;
tel. 020 7401 2077; fax 020 7633 9499

www.southwaterbooks.com; www.annesspublishing.com

If you like the images in this book and would like to investigate using them for publishing, promotions
or advertising, please visit our website www.practicalpictures.com for more information.

UK agent: The Manning Partnership Ltd;
tel. 01225 478444; fax 01225 478440;
sales@manning-partnership.co.uk
UK distributor: Grantham Book Services Ltd;
tel. 01476 541080; fax 01476 541061;
orders@gbs.tbs-ltd.co.uk
North American agent/distributor:
National Book Network;
tel. 301 459 3366; fax 301 429 5746;
www.nbnbooks.com

Australian agent/distributor:
Pan Macmillan Australia;
tel. 1300 135 113; fax 1300 135 103;
customer.service@macmillan.com.au
New Zealand agent/distributor:
David Bateman Ltd;
tel. (09) 415 7664; fax (09) 415 8892

Main front cover image shows Linguine
with Crab – for recipe, see page 69

Publisher: Joanna Lorenz
Managing Editor: Judith Simons
Project Editor: Mariano Kälfors
Consultant Editor: Anne Sheasby
Nutritional Analysis: Jill Scott
Recipes: Catherine Atkinson, Carla Capalbo, Kit Chan, Jacqueline Clarke, Maxine Clarke, Frances Cleary, Carol Clements, Roz Denny, Matthew Drennan,
Joanna Farrow, Christine France, Sarah Gates, Shirley Gill, Carole Handslip, Christine Ingram, Patricia Lousada, Norma MacMillan, Sue Maggs,
Elizabeth Martin, Sarah Maxwell, Janice Murfitt, Annie Nichols, Angela Nilsen, Maggie Pannell, Louise Pickford, Jennie Shapter, Anne Sheasby,
Hilaire Walden, Laura Washburn, Steven Wheeler, Kate Whiteman, Judy Williams, Elizabeth Wolf-Cohen, Jeni Wright
Photographers: Karl Adamson, Edward Allwright, David Armstrong, Steve Baxter, Nicki Dowey, James Duncan, Michelle Garrett, Amanda Heywood,
David Jordan, Dave King, Don Last, William Lingwood, Patrick McLeavey, Michael Michaels, Thomas Odulate, Peter Reilly.
Designers: Nigel Partridge, Ian Sandom
Production Controller: Pirong Wang

ETHICAL TRADING POLICY
Because of our ongoing ecological investment programme, you, as our customer, can have the pleasure and reassurance of knowing
that a tree is being cultivated on your behalf to naturally replace the materials used to make the book you are holding.
For further information about this scheme, go to www.annesspublishing.com/trees

A CIP catalogue record for this book is available from the British Library.

NOTES
Bracketed terms are intended for American readers.

For all recipes, quantities are given in both metric and imperial measures and, where appropriate, in standard cups and spoons.
Follow one set of measures, but not a mixture, because they are not interchangeable.

Standard spoon and cup measures are level. 1 tsp = 5ml, 1 tbsp = 15ml, 1 cup = 250ml/8fl oz.
Australian standard tablespoons are 20ml. Australian readers should use 3 tsp in place of 1 tbsp for measuring small quantities.

American pints are 16fl oz/2 cups. American readers should use 20fl oz/2.5 cups in place of 1 pint when measuring liquids.

Electric oven temperatures in this book are for conventional ovens. When using a fan oven, the temperature will probably need to be reduced
by about 10–20°C/20–40°F. Since ovens vary, you should check with your manufacturer's instruction book for guidance.

The nutritional analysis given for each recipe is calculated per portion (i.e. serving or item), unless otherwise stated. If the recipe gives a range, such as Serves 4–6,
then the nutritional analysis will be for the smaller portion size, i.e. 6 servings. Measurements for sodium do not include salt added to taste.

Medium (US large) eggs are used unless otherwise stated.

PUBLISHER'S NOTE
Although the advice and information in this book are believed to be accurate and true at the time of going to press, neither the
authors nor the publisher can accept any legal responsibility or liability for any errors or omissions that may be made.

CONTENTS

INTRODUCTION 6
HEALTHY EATING GUIDELINES 8
EASY WAYS TO CUT DOWN ON FAT
AND SATURATED FAT IN THE DAILY DIET 10
FAT-FREE COOKING METHODS 11
TYPES OF PASTA 12
TECHNIQUES 14

PASTA SOUPS AND SALADS 18

MEAT AND POULTRY PASTA DISHES 36

FISH AND SHELLFISH PASTA DISHES 52

VEGETARIAN PASTA DISHES 72

INDEX 96

INTRODUCTION

Modern nutritional research has demonstrated the value of starchy foods. These carbohydrates release energy slowly at an even rate, avoiding the sudden highs and lows of sugary foods. They are an important source of dietary fibre, which as well as aiding the function of the digestive system, also provides a feeling of fullness and satisfaction. Other research has shown that a Mediterranean diet, with its emphasis on fresh fruit and vegetables, prominence of fish and white meat and widespread use of olive oil, is one of the healthiest in the world. Put these together and you have the perfect combination of pasta and low-fat sauces and what is more, you have a truly delicious, as well as a healthy meal.

Naturally low in fat, pasta forms the perfect basis for a healthy diet. It is immensely versatile and combines superbly with a wide range of other ingredients, such as vegetables, mushrooms, poultry, meat, fish and shellfish. Many traditional Italian pasta recipes are already low in saturated fats and heavier, richer dishes can be adapted easily to modern tastes and requirements. For example, typical Italian ingredients, such as pancetta, salami and mozzarella, are high in fat, but are easily replaced with lower-fat foods, such as lean bacon and reduced-fat cheese. Equally, in many recipes, the quantity of a high-fat ingredient can be reduced to lower the overall fat content of the dish.

It is also worth bearing in mind the first guiding rule of all Italian cooks, use only the best-quality ingredients. So, although the best Parmesan cheese, for example, may be high in fat, it is so flavoursome that only a small quantity is required. The second rule is to let the natural flavours of the high-quality ingredients lead the way. Simple methods of cooking are often the tastiest – lightly grilled (broiled) chicken, flavoured with herbs and spices is at least as delicious and certainly much healthier than a dish smothered in an elaborate cream sauce.

BELOW: Pasta forms a wonderful basis and combines superbly with other ingredients for a low fat dish packed full of flavour.

ABOVE: Fish and shellfish such as sardines and mussels are nutritious, low in fat and ideal for creating delicious pasta dishes.

Many traditional Italian foods, such as an abundance of sun-ripened vegetables and fresh herbs, are naturally low in fat, making them ideal to enjoy as part of a low-fat eating plan. Olive oil is the primary fat used for cooking throughout the Mediterranean. It is a "healthier" oil because it contains a high proportion of monounsaturated fat and is low in saturated fats, as well as being a good source of vitamin A. It has been shown to help lower levels of cholesterol in the blood and, so long as it is used in moderation, it can be enjoyed as part of a low-fat diet. It also has an incomparable flavour. The recipes in this book also recommend using other "healthy" oils, such as sunflower and rapeseed (canola), when a blander flavour is required.

Most of us eat fats in some form or another every day and we all need a small amount of fat in our diet to maintain a healthy, balanced eating plan. It would be unwise – and probably impossible – to cut out fats all together. However, most of us eat far too much fat and we should all be looking to reduce our overall fat

intake, and especially the quantity of saturated fat. Weight for weight, dietary fats supply far more energy than all the other nutrients in our diet and if you eat foods that are high in fat, but don't exercise sufficiently to use up that energy, you will gain weight and render yourself more susceptible to a number of illnesses.

By cutting down on the amount of fat you eat and making easy changes to your diet, such as choosing the right types of fat, using low-fat and fat-free products whenever possible and modifying the way you prepare and cook food, you will soon be reducing your overall fat intake and enjoying a much healthier lifestyle – and you will hardly notice the difference.

As you will see from this book, it is certainly practicable to eat and enjoy pasta as part of a low-fat eating plan. We include lots of useful and informative advice, including an introduction to basic healthy eating guidelines, helpful hints on low-fat and fat-free ingredients and low-fat or fat-free cooking techniques and practical tips on how to reduce fat, especially saturated fat, in your diet. In addition, there is a useful guide to types

RIGHT: A selection of flavourings essential for pasta dishes.

of pasta and how to cook and serve it to perfection, as well as step-by-step instructions for making your own dough and preparing your different pasta shapes.

Each of the delicious, low-fat recipes includes a nutritional breakdown, providing an at-a-glance calorie and fat contents per serving. All the recipes in this cookbook are very low in fat – none of them containing more than five grams of fat per serving and some of them containing less than one gram of fat per serving.

You will be surprised and delighted at this tempting collection of recipes which ranges from soups and salads to main course meat, fish and vegetarian pasta dishes. Many of the recipes are based on traditional Italian dishes and, even though they contain less fat, are packed full of flavour and appeal. This practical book will give you a valuable insight into low-fat pasta cooking and will enable you to enjoy healthy, nutritious and, above all, delicious food with all the pleasure of a clear conscience.

HEALTHY EATING GUIDELINES

A healthy diet is one that provides us with all the nutrients we need. By eating the right types, balance and proportions of foods, we are more likely to feel healthy, have plenty of energy and a higher resistance to disease that will help prevent us from developing illnesses, such as heart disease, cancers, bowel disorders and obesity.

By choosing a variety of foods every day, you will ensure that you are supplying your body with all the essential nutrients, including vitamins and minerals, it needs. To get the balance right, it is important to know just how much of each type of food you should be eating.

There are five main food groups, and it is recommended that we should eat plenty of fruit and vegetables (at least five portions a day, not including potatoes) and foods such as pasta, cereals, rice and potatoes; moderate amounts of meat, fish, poultry and dairy products, and only small amounts of foods containing fat or sugar. By choosing a good balance of foods from these groups every day, and by choosing lower-fat or lower-sugar alternatives, we will be supplying our bodies with all the nutrients they need for optimum health.

THE FIVE MAIN FOOD GROUPS

- Fruit and vegetables
- Pasta, rice, potatoes, bread and other cereals
- Meat, poultry, fish and alternative proteins, such as peas, beans and lentils
- Milk and other dairy foods
- Foods that contain fat and foods that contain sugar

THE ROLE AND IMPORTANCE OF FAT IN OUR DIET

Fats shouldn't be cut out of our diets completely. We need a small amount of fat for general health and well-being – fat is a valuable source of energy, and also helps to make foods more palatable to eat. However, if you lower the fats, especially saturated fats, in your diet, it may help you to lose weight as well as reducing your risk of developing some diseases, such as heart disease.

Aim to limit your daily intake of fats to no more than 30–35 per cent of the total number of calories. Since each gram of fat provides nine calories, your total daily intake should be no more than around 70g fat. Your total intake of saturated fats should be no more than approximately ten per cent of the total number of calories.

ABOVE: By choosing a variety of foods from the five main food groups, you will ensure that you are supplying your body with all the nutrients it needs.

TYPES OF FAT

All fats in our foods are made up of building blocks of fatty acids and glycerol and their properties vary according to each combination.

There are two main types of fat, which are referred to as saturated and unsaturated. The unsaturated group of fats is divided into two further types: polyunsaturated and monounsaturated fats.

There is usually a combination of these types of fat (saturated, polyunsaturated and monounsaturated) in foods that contain fat, but the amount of each type varies from one kind of food to another.

SATURATED FATS

These fats are usually hard at room temperature. They are not essential in the diet, and should be limited, as they are linked to increasing the level of cholesterol in the blood, which in turn can increase the likelihood that heart disease will develop.

The main sources of saturated fats are animal products, such as fatty meats, and spreading fats, such as butter and lard, that are solid at room temperature. However, there are also saturated fats of vegetable origin, notably coconut and

BELOW: A selection of foods containing the three main types of fat: saturated, polyunsaturated and monounsaturated fats. Small quantities of poly- and monounsaturated fats can help to reduce the level of cholesterol in the blood.

palm oils, and some margarines and oils, which, when processed, change the nature of the fat from unsaturated fatty acids to saturated ones. These fats are labelled "hydrogenated vegetable oil" and should be limited. Saturated fats are also found in many processed foods, such as savoury snacks, as well as biscuits (cookies) and cakes.

POLYUNSATURATED FATS

There are two types of polyunsaturated fats: those of vegetable or plant origin (omega 6), such as sunflower oil, soft margarine and seeds, and those from oily fish (omega 3), such as salmon, herring, mackerel and sardines. Both fats are usually liquid at room temperature. Small quantities of polyunsaturated fats are essential for good health and are thought to help reduce the blood cholesterol level.

MONOUNSATURATED FATS

Monounsaturated fats are also thought to have the beneficial effect of reducing the blood cholesterol level and this could explain why in some Mediterranean countries there is such a low incidence of heart disease. Monounsaturated fats are found in foods such as olive oil, rapeseed (canola) oil, some nuts such as almonds and hazelnuts, oily fish and avocados.

CUTTING DOWN ON FATS AND SATURATED FATS IN THE DIET

About one-quarter of the fat we eat comes from meat and meat products, one-fifth from dairy products and margarine and the rest from cakes, biscuits, pastries and other foods.

It is relatively easy to cut down on obvious sources of fat in the diet, such as butter, oils, margarine, cream, whole milk and full-fat cheese, but we also need to know about – and check our consumption of – "hidden" fats. Hidden fats can be found in foods such as cakes, crisps (US chips), biscuits and nuts.

By being aware of which foods are high in fats and particularly saturated fats, and by making simple changes to your diet, you can reduce the total fat content of your diet quite considerably.

Whenever possible, choose reduced-fat or low-fat alternatives to foods such as milk, cheese and salad dressings, and fill up on very low-fat foods, such as fruit and vegetables, and foods that are high in carbohydrates, such rice, bread, potatoes and, of course, pasta.

Cutting down on fat doesn't mean sacrificing taste. It's easy to follow a healthy-eating plan without having to forgo all your favourite foods.

EASY WAYS TO CUT DOWN ON FAT AND SATURATED FAT IN THE DAILY DIET

—

There are lots of simple no-fuss ways of reducing the fat in your diet. Just follow the simple "eat less – try instead" suggestions below to discover how easy it is.

• EAT LESS – Butter, margarine, other spreading fats and cooking oils.

• TRY INSTEAD – Low-fat spread or very low-fat spread. If you must use butter or hard margarine, make sure they are softened at room temperature so that you can spread them very thinly, or try fat-free spreads. Bread for mopping up sauce doesn't really require a spread.

• EAT LESS – Fatty meats and high-fat products, such as meat pâtés and burgers.

• TRY INSTEAD – Low-fat meats, such as chicken, turkey and venison. Use only the leanest cuts of meats such as lamb, beef and pork. Always cut and discard any visible fat and skin from meat before cooking. Follow the Italian custom of making a little meat go a long way in a pasta sauce, and eat fish more often. Try using low-fat protein products such as peas, beans, lentils or beancurd (tofu) in place of meat in recipes.

• EAT LESS – Full-fat dairy products such as whole milk, cream, butter, hard

BELOW: Chicken and fish are low in fat; always use only the leanest cuts of meats.

ABOVE: Look for reduced-fat hard cheeses, low-fat yogurts and skimmed milk.

margarine, crème fraîche, whole milk yogurts and hard cheese.

• TRY INSTEAD – Semi-skimmed (low-fat) or skimmed milk and milk products, low-fat yogurts, low-fat fromage frais and low-fat soft cheeses, reduced-fat hard cheeses such as Cheddar, and reduced-fat creams and crème fraîche.

• EAT LESS – Hard cooking fats, such as lard or hard margarine.

• TRY INSTEAD – Polyunsaturated or monounsaturated oils, such as olive, sunflower or corn oil for cooking (but don't use too much).

• EAT LESS – Rich salad dressings, such as full-fat mayonnaise, salad cream or French dressing.

• TRY INSTEAD – Reduced-fat or fat-free mayonnaise or dressings. Make salad dressings at home with low-fat yogurt, fromage frais or soft cheese.

• EAT LESS – Fried foods.

• TRY INSTEAD – Fat-free cooking methods such as grilling (broiling), poaching, steaming or baking whenever

possible. Try cooking in a non-stick frying pan with only a very small amount of oil. Always grill (broil) meat or poultry on a rack, so the fat drains away.

• EAT LESS – Deep-fried chips (french fries) and sautéed potatoes.

• TRY INSTEAD – Low-fat starchy foods, such as pasta, which release energy slowly and over a period of time, leaving you satisfied for longer.

• EAT LESS – Added fat in cooking.

• TRY INSTEAD – To cook with little or no fat. Use heavy-based or good quality non-stick pans so that the food doesn't stick. Try using a small amount of spray oil in cooking to control exactly how much fat you are using. Use fat-free or low-fat ingredients for cooking, such as low-fat or fat-free stock, wine or even beer.

• EAT LESS – High-fat snacks, such as crisps (US chips), tortilla chips, fried snacks and pastries.

• TRY INSTEAD – Low-fat and fat-free fresh or dried fruits, breadsticks or vegetable sticks. Eating plenty of carbohydrate, such as pasta, for lunch or supper, ensures a steady release of energy, so you will require fewer snacks.

BELOW: Aromatic herbs add depth of flavour and interest to low-fat recipes.

FAT-FREE COOKING METHODS

It's extremely easy to cook without fat – whenever possible, grill, bake, poach and steam foods without the addition of fat, or try stir-frying without fat – try using a little low-fat or fat-free stock or red or white wine instead.

• By choosing heavy-based or good quality cookware, you'll find that the amount of fat needed for cooking foods can be kept to an absolute minimum. When making meat sauces such as Bolognese, dry fry the meat to brown it and then drain off all the excess fat before adding the other ingredients. If you do need a little fat for cooking, choose an oil that is high in unsaturates, such as corn, sunflower, olive or rapeseed (canola) oil, and always use as little as possible.

• When baking pasta dishes, use good quality bakeware which doesn't need greasing before use, or use non-stick baking parchment and only lightly grease before lining.

• Look out for non-stick coated fabric sheet. This re-usable non-stick material is amazingly versatile. It can be cut to size and used to line baking sheets or frying pans. Heat-resistant up to

BELOW: Always cut off and discard visible fat and skin from meat before cooking.

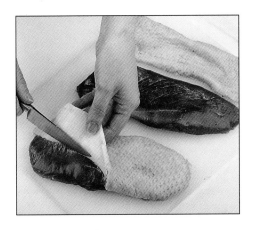

ABOVE: Marinating helps to tenderize meat as well as adding flavour and colour.

290°C/550°F and microwave-safe, it will last for up to five years.

• When baking foods such as chicken or fish, rather than adding a knob (pat) of butter to the food, try baking it in a loosely sealed parcel of foil or greaseproof (waxed) paper and adding some wine and herbs or spices for extra flavouring before sealing the parcel.

• When grilling (broiling) foods, the addition of fat is often unnecessary. If the food shows signs of drying, lightly brush with a small amount of unsaturated oil, such as sunflower or corn oil.

• Microwaved foods rarely need the addition of fat, so add herbs or spices for extra flavour and colour.

• Steaming or boiling are easy, fat-free ways of cooking many foods, especially vegetables, fish and chicken, the delicate texture of which responds well to this cooking technique.

• Try poaching foods, such as chicken and fish, in low-fat or fat-free stock – it is another easy, fat-free cooking method.

• Try braising vegetables in the oven in low-fat or fat-free stock, wine, cider, fruit juice or simply water with the addition of some herbs.

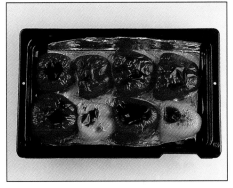

ABOVE: Vegetables can be grilled (broiled) without adding any fat at all.

• Sauté vegetables in low-fat or fat-free stock, wine or even fruit juice instead of oil.

• Cook vegetables in a covered pan over a low heat with a little water so they cook in their own juices. This also helps to preserve vitamins and other nutrients.

• Marinate food such as meat or poultry in mixtures of alcohol, herbs or spices, and vinegar or fruit juice. This will help to tenderize the meat and add flavour and colour. In addition, the leftover marinade can be used to baste the food occasionally while it is cooking or added to the sauce for extra flavour.

LOW-FAT SPREADS IN COOKING

There is a huge variety of low-fat, reduced-fat and half-fat spreads available in our supermarkets, along with some spreads that are very low in fat. Generally speaking, the very low-fat spreads with a fat content of around 20 per cent or less have a high water content and so are unsuitable for cooking and only suitable for spreading.

TYPES OF PASTA

Pasta is the one ingredient that probably sums up the essence of Italian cooking, and it is an essential part of many Italian meals. It is a wonderfully simple, nutritious and low-fat food which is available in a whole wealth of shapes and sizes. There are two basic types of pasta, dried and fresh.

FRESH PASTA

Home-made fresh pasta is usually made by hand using superfine plain (all-purpose) white flour enriched with eggs. It is often wrapped around a low-fat stuffing of lean meat, fish, vegetables or low-fat cheese to make filled pasta, such as ravioli or tortellini, or layered with lean meat or vegetable sauces to make a tasty low-fat lasagne. Commercially made fresh pasta is made with durum wheat, water and eggs. The flavour and texture of all fresh pasta is very delicate, so it is best suited to slightly creamier, low-fat sauces.

DRIED PASTA

Dried pasta is produced from a dough made from hard durum wheat. It is then shaped into numerous different forms, from long, thin spaghetti to elaborate spirals and frilly bow shapes. Dried pasta can be made from basic pasta dough, which consists of durum wheat and water, or it can be made from a dough enriched with eggs

LEFT: Dried rigatoni

ABOVE: Fresh pasta comes in a wide variety of interesting shapes, sizes and colours.

LEFT: Angel's hair pasta

RIGHT: Fettuccine

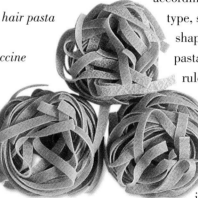

or coloured and flavoured with ingredients such as spinach, herbs, tomatoes or squid ink. Dried pasta has a nutty flavour and should always retain a firm texture when cooked. It is generally used in preference to fresh pasta for thinner-textured, more robust, low-fat sauces.

BUYING AND STORING PASTA

Choose dried pasta that is made from durum wheat and store it in a cool, dry place. Once opened, dried pasta will keep for weeks in an airtight container. Home-made fresh pasta will keep for only a couple of days, but it also freezes very well. Commercially made fresh pasta is

RIGHT: Dried spaghetti

pasteurized and vacuum-packed, so it will keep in the refrigerator for about two weeks, or it can be frozen for up to six months. When buying coloured and flavoured pasta, make sure that it has been made with natural ingredients.

COOKING PASTA

All pasta must be cooked in a large pan filled with plenty of fast-boiling, salted water. Cooking times vary according to the type, size and shape of the pasta but, as a general rule, filled pasta takes about 12 minutes, dried pasta needs 8–10 minutes and fresh pasta only 2–3 minutes. All pasta should be cooked until it is *al dente*, or still firm to the bite. Always test pasta for readiness just before you think it should be done as it can easily overcook. To stop it cooking, take the pan off the heat and run a little cold water into it, then drain the pasta and serve.

PASTA VARIETIES

Pasta shapes can be divided roughly into four categories: long strands or ribbons, flat, short and filled. When choosing the appropriate pasta for a sauce, there are no hard-and-fast rules; almost any pasta is suitable for a low-fat sauce.

LEFT: Conchiglie

BELOW: Tomato and spinach orecchiette

SHORT PASTA

Short pasta covers a wide variety of shapes, the more common types are macaroni, rigati, rigatoni and tubetti. Pasta shapes vary and the list is almost endless, with some wonderfully descriptive names. There are cappellacci (little hats), orecchiette (little ears) or maltagliati (badly cut) and penne (quills), conchiglie (little shells), farfalle (bows) and lumache (snails).

LONG OR RIBBON PASTA

The best-known long variety is spaghetti, which also comes in a thinner version, spaghettini, and the flatter linguine, which means "little tongues". Bucatini are thicker and hollow – perfect for trapping low-fat sauces in the cavity. Ribbon pasta is wider than the strands and fettuccine, tagliatelle and trenette all fall into this category. Dried tagliatelle is usually sold folded into nests, which unravel during cooking. Pappardelle are the widest ribbon pasta; they are often served with a low-fat rabbit sauce. The thinnest pasta strands are vermicelli (little worms) and ultra-fine capelli d'angelo (angel's hair).

FLAT PASTA

In Italy, fresh flat pasta is often called maccheroni, not to be confused with the short tubes of macaroni with which we are familiar. Lasagne and cannelloni are larger flat rectangles of pasta, used for layering or rolling round a low-fat filling; dried cannelloni are already formed into wide tubes. Layered pasta dishes like this are cooked in the oven.

RIGHT: Lasagne

BELOW: Multi-coloured tagliatelle

RIGHT: Tortellini

FILLED PASTA

Dried and fresh filled pastas are available in many varieties and there are dozens of names for filled pasta, but the only difference lies in the shape and size. Ravioli are square, tortelli and agnolotti are usually round, while tortellini and anellini are ring-shaped. Fillings for fresh and dried pasta include lean meat, pumpkin, artichokes, ricotta and spinach, seafood, chicken and mushrooms.

GNOCCHI

Gnocchi fall into a different category from other pasta, being similar to small dumplings. They can be made from semolina (milled durum wheat), flour, potatoes or ricotta and spinach and may be shaped like elongated shells, ovals, cylinders or flat discs, or roughly shredded into strozzapreti (priest stranglers). Gnocchi are extremely light and almost melt in the mouth and can be served like any pasta, as a low-fat first course, in clear soup or as part of a main course.

RIGHT: Gnocchi

TECHNIQUES

MAKING BASIC PASTA DOUGH ON A WORK SURFACE

The best place to make, knead and roll out pasta dough is on a wooden kitchen table – the larger the better. The surface should be warm, so marble is not suitable.

INGREDIENTS
200g/7oz/1¾ cups plain (all-purpose) flour
pinch of salt
2 eggs
10ml/2 tsp cold water

SERVES 3–4

VARIATIONS
TOMATO: add 20ml/4 tsp concentrated tomato purée (paste) to the eggs before mixing.
SPINACH: add 115g/4oz frozen spinach, thawed and squeezed dry. Blend with the eggs, before adding to the flour.
HERB: add 45ml/3 tbsp finely chopped fresh herbs to the eggs before mixing.

1 Sift the flour and salt on to a clean work surface and make a well in the centre with your hand.

2 Put the eggs and water into the well. Using a fork, beat the eggs gently together, then gradually draw in the flour from the sides, to make a thick paste.

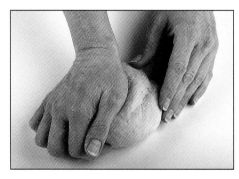

3 When the mixture becomes too stiff to use a fork, use your hands to mix to a firm dough. Knead the dough for about 5 minutes, until smooth. (This can be done in an electric food mixer fitted with a dough hook.) Wrap in clear film (plastic wrap) to prevent it drying out and leave to rest for 20–30 minutes.

MAKING BASIC PASTA DOUGH IN A BOWL

1 Sift the flour and salt into a glass bowl and make a well in the centre. Add the eggs and water.

2 Using a fork, beat the eggs gently together, then gradually draw in the flour from the sides, to make a thick paste.

3 When the mixture becomes too stiff to use a fork, use your hands to mix to a firm dough. Knead the dough for 5 minutes until smooth. (This can be done in an electric food mixer fitted with a dough hook.) Wrap in clear film (plastic wrap) and leave for 20–30 minutes.

ROLLING OUT PASTA DOUGH BY HAND

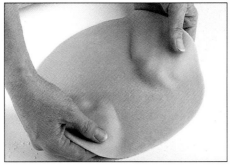

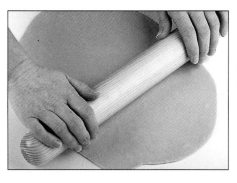

1 Cut the basic dough into quarters. Use one quarter at a time and re-wrap the rest in clear film (plastic wrap) so it does not dry out. Flatten the dough and dust liberally with flour. Start rolling out the dough, making sure you roll it evenly.

2 As the dough becomes thinner, keep on rotating it on the work surface by gently lifting the edges with your fingers and supporting it over the rolling pin. Make sure you don't tear the dough.

3 Carry on rolling out the dough until it has reached the desired thickness, about 3mm/⅛in thick.

ROLLING OUT DOUGH USING A PASTA MACHINE

1 Cut the basic dough into quarters. Use one quarter at a time and re-wrap the rest in clear film (plastic wrap) so it does not dry out. Flatten the dough and dust liberally with flour. Start with the machine set to roll at the thickest setting. Pass the dough through the rollers several times, dusting the dough from time to time with flour until it is smooth.

2 Fold the strip of dough into three, press the joins well together and pass through the machine again. Repeat the folding and rolling several times on each setting.

3 Guide the dough through the machine but do not pull or stretch it or the dough will tear. As the dough is worked through all the settings, it will become thinner and longer. Guide the dough over your hand, as the dough is rolled out to a thin sheet. Pasta used for stuffing, such as ravioli or tortellini, should be used straightaway. Otherwise lay the rolled sheets on a clean dishtowel, lightly dusted with sifted flour, and leave to dry for 10 minutes before cutting. This makes it easier to cut and prevents the strands of pasta sticking together.

CUTTING PASTA SHAPES

Until you are confident at handling and shaping pasta dough, it is easier to work with small
quantities. Always keep the dough well wrapped to prevent it from drying out, before
you are ready to work with it.

CUTTING OUT TAGLIATELLE

To cut tagliatelle, fit the appropriate
attachment to the machine or move the
handle to the appropriate slot. Cut the
pasta sheets into 25cm/10in lengths
and pass these through the machine.
Guide the strands over the back of your
hand as they appear out of the machine.

CUTTING OUT LASAGNE

Take a sheet of pasta dough and cut out
neat rectangles about 18×7.5cm/7×3in
to make sheets of lasagne. Lay on a clean
dishtowel to dry.

CUTTING OUT SPAGHETTI

To cut spaghetti, fit the appropriate
attachment to the machine or move the
handle to the appropriate slot. Cut the
pasta sheets into 25cm/10in lengths and
pass these through the machine as
for tagliatelle.

SHAPING RAVIOLI

Ravioli made in this way are not perfectly square, but they look charmingly home-made.

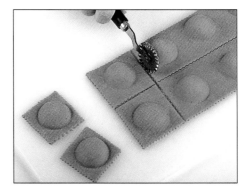

1 To make ravioli, place spoonfuls of
filling on a sheet of dough at intervals of
5–7.5cm/2–3in, leaving a 2.5cm/1in
border. Brush the dough between the
spoonfuls of filling with lightly beaten
egg white.

2 Lay a second sheet of pasta carefully
over the top. Press around each mound of
filling, excluding any air pockets.

3 Using a fluted pastry wheel or a sharp
knife, cut between the stuffing to make
square-shaped parcels.

MAKING FARFALLE (PASTA BOWS)

1 Roll the pasta dough through a pasta machine until the sheets are very thin. Then cut into long strips 4cm/1½in wide.

2 Cut the strips into small rectangles. Run a pastry wheel along the two shorter edges of the little rectangles – this will give the bows a decorative edge.

3 Moisten the centre of the strips and using a finger and thumb, gently pinch each rectangle together in the middle to make little pasta bows.

MAKING TAGLIATELLE

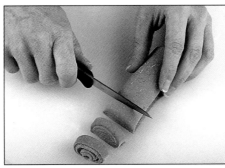

1 Lightly flour some spinach-flavoured pasta dough, cut into a rectangle 30 × 10cm/12 × 4in and roll it up.

2 Using a sharp knife, cut straight across the pasta roll.

3 Carefully unravel each little roll as you cut it to make ribbons of fresh tagliatelle.

COOKING PASTA

1 Before starting to cook either the sauce or pasta, read through the recipe carefully. It is important to know which needs to be cooked for the longest time – sometimes it is the pasta and sometimes the sauce, so don't always assume one or the other. The sauce can often be made ahead of time and reheated, but pasta is almost like a hot soufflé – it waits for no one.

2 There needs to be plenty of room for the pasta to move around in the large amount of water it requires, so a large pan is essential. The best type of pan is a tall, lightweight, straight-sided, stainless steel pasta cooking pot with its own in-built draining pan. Both outer and inner pans have two handles each, which ensures easy and safe lifting and draining. It is well worth investing in one of these pans.

3 Use a large quantity of water. If there is not enough water, the pasta shapes will stick together as they swell and the pan will become overcrowded. This will result in gummy-textured pasta. Before adding the pasta, the water should be at a fast rolling boil. The quickest way to do this is to boil water in a kettle, then pour it into the pasta pan, which should be set over high heat.

PASTA SOUPS AND SALADS

This APPETIZING *array of low-fat soups and salads provides tempting dishes to launch a meal or make a complete* LIGHT *meal on their own. We include a selection of home-made* LOW-FAT *soups, such as* VEGETABLE *Minestrone, Chicken and Pasta Soup and Roasted* TOMATO *and Pasta Soup. Choose also from* PASTA *salads such as Duck and Pasta Salad and Farfalle Salad with Piquant* PEPPERS.

PUGLIA-STYLE MINESTRONE

This is a tasty low-fat soup for a supper early in the week because it can be made with the leftover carcass of Sunday's roast chicken.

INGREDIENTS

1 roast chicken carcass
1 onion, quartered lengthways
1 carrot, roughly chopped
1 celery stick, roughly chopped
a few black peppercorns
1 small handful mixed fresh herbs, such as parsley and thyme
1 chicken stock (bouillon) cube
50g/2oz/1/2 cup dried tubetti
salt and freshly ground black pepper
25g/1oz ricotta salata or feta cheese, coarsely grated or crumbled, and 30ml/ 2 tbsp fresh mint leaves, to serve

SERVES 4

1 Break the chicken carcass into pieces and place these in a large pan. Add the onion, carrot, celery, peppercorns and fresh herbs, then crumble in the stock cube and add a good pinch of salt. Cover the chicken generously with cold water (you will need about 1.5 litres/2½ pints/ 6¼ cups) and bring to the boil over a high heat.

2 Reduce the heat, half cover the pan and simmer gently for about 1 hour. Remove the pan from the heat and leave the mixture to cool, then strain the liquid through a colander or sieve into a clean, large pan.

3 Remove any meat from the chicken bones, cut it into bitesize pieces and set aside. Discard the carcass and all the flavouring ingredients.

4 Bring the stock in the pan to the boil, add the pasta and simmer, stirring frequently for 5–6 minutes, or according to the packet instructions, until only just tender or *al dente*.

5 Add the chicken and heat through for a few minutes, by which time the pasta will be ready. Adjust the seasoning. Serve hot in soup bowls, sprinkled with the ricotta salata or feta cheese and mint leaves.

NUTRITIONAL NOTES
Per portion:

Energy	59Kcals/250kJ
Total fat	1.5g
Saturated fat	0.9g
Cholesterol	4.38mg
Fibre	0.4g

VEGETABLE MINESTRONE

—

This vegetable and pasta soup makes a tasty appetizer or snack dish
which is very low in fat.

3 Add the tomatoes, the saffron with its liquid and the frozen peas. Bring back to the boil and add the soup pasta. Simmer for 10 minutes until tender or *al dente*, stirring occasionally.

4 Season with sugar, salt and pepper to taste. Stir in the chopped herbs just before serving. Ladle into soup bowls and serve.

INGREDIENTS

large pinch of saffron threads
1 onion, chopped
1 leek, sliced
1 celery stick, sliced
2 carrots, diced
2–3 garlic cloves, crushed
600ml/1 pint/2¹/₂ cups chicken stock
2 x 400g/14oz cans chopped tomatoes
50g/2oz/¹/₂ cup frozen peas
50g/2oz/¹/₂ cup dried soup pasta,
such as anellini
5ml/1 tsp caster (superfine) sugar
15ml/1 tbsp chopped fresh parsley
15ml/1 tbsp chopped fresh basil
salt and freshly ground black pepper

SERVES 4

1 Soak the saffron threads in 15ml/1 tbsp boiling water in a small bowl. Leave to stand for 10 minutes.

2 Meanwhile, put the onion, leek, celery, carrots and garlic into a large pan. Add the chicken stock, bring to the boil, cover and simmer for about 10 minutes.

NUTRITIONAL NOTES
Per portion:

Energy	77Kcals/330kJ
Total fat	0.6g
Saturated fat	0.1g
Cholesterol	0mg
Fibre	2.9g

LITTLE STUFFED HATS IN BROTH

This soup is served in northern Italy on Santo Stefano (St Stephen's Day – the day after Christmas). It makes a light change from all the celebration food the day before.

INGREDIENTS
1.2 litres/2 pints/5 cups chicken stock
90–115g/3½–4oz/1 cup fresh or
dried cappelletti
30ml/2 tbsp dry white wine (optional)
about 15ml/1 tbsp finely chopped fresh flat
leaf parsley (optional)
salt and freshly ground black pepper
shredded flat leaf parsley, to garnish
15ml/1 tbsp grated fresh Parmesan cheese,
to serve

SERVES 4

1 Pour the chicken stock into a large pan and bring to the boil. Add a little salt and pepper to taste.

2 Drop in the pasta, stir well and bring back to the boil. Reduce the heat to a simmer and cook, according to the packet instructions, until the pasta is tender or *al dente*. Stir the pasta frequently during cooking to ensure that it cooks evenly.

3 Swirl in the wine and parsley, if using, then adjust the seasoning. Ladle into warmed soup bowls, then sprinkle with shredded flat leaf parsley and grated Parmesan. Serve immediately.

NUTRITIONAL NOTES
Per portion:

Energy	103Kcals/436kJ
Total fat	1.7g
Saturated fat	0.8g
Cholesterol	3.7mg
Fibre	0.8g

TINY PASTA IN BROTH

In Italy this tasty pasta soup is often served with bread for a light evening supper or for a quick midday snack. You can use any other dried tiny soup pastas in place of the funghetti.

INGREDIENTS
1.2 litres/2 pints/5 cups beef stock
75g/3oz/¾ cup dried tiny soup pasta,
such as funghetti
2 pieces bottled roasted red (bell) pepper,
about 50g/2oz
salt and freshly ground black pepper
25g/1oz coarsely shaved fresh Parmesan
cheese, to serve

SERVES 4

1 Bring the beef stock to the boil in a large pan. Add salt and pepper to taste, then drop in the dried soup pasta. Stir well and bring the stock back to the boil.

2 Reduce the heat to a simmer and cook for 7–8 minutes, or according to the packet instructions, until the pasta is tender or *al dente*. Stir frequently during cooking to prevent the pasta shapes from sticking together.

NUTRITIONAL NOTES
Per portion:

Energy	108Kcals/457kJ
Total fat	3.7g
Saturated fat	1.5g
Cholesterol	6.2mg
Fibre	0.8g

3 Drain the pieces of roasted pepper and dice them finely. Place them in the bottom of 4 soup bowls. Taste the soup and adjust the seasoning. Ladle into the soup bowls and serve immediately, with shavings of Parmesan served separately.

PASTA AND CHICKPEA SOUP

—

A simple, country-style soup, ideal for a flavourful, low-fat starter. You can use other pasta shapes, but conchiglie are ideal because they scoop up the chickpeas and beans.

INGREDIENTS

1 onion
2 carrots
2 celery sticks
15ml/1 tbsp olive oil
400g/14oz can chickpeas, rinsed and drained
200g/7oz can cannellini beans, rinsed and drained
150ml/¹/4 pint/²/3 cup passata (bottled strained tomatoes)
120ml/4fl oz/¹/2 cup water
1.5 litres/2¹/2 pints/6¹/4 cups chicken stock
1 fresh or dried rosemary sprig
200g/7oz/scant 2 cups dried conchiglie
salt and freshly ground black pepper
fresh rosemary leaves, to garnish
15ml/1 tbsp grated fresh Parmesan cheese, to serve

SERVES 6

1 Chop the onion, carrots and celery sticks finely, either in a food processor or by hand.

2 Heat the olive oil in a large, heavy pan, add the chopped vegetables and cook over a low heat, stirring frequently, for 5–7 minutes.

3 Add the chickpeas and cannellini beans, stir well to mix, then cook for 5 minutes. Stir in the passata and water. Cook, stirring, for 2–3 minutes.

4 Add 475ml/16fl oz/2 cups of the stock, the rosemary sprig and salt and pepper to taste. Bring to the boil, cover, then simmer gently, stirring occasionally, for 1 hour.

NUTRITIONAL NOTES
Per portion:

Energy	201Kcals/849kJ
Total fat	4.5g
Saturated fat	0.9g
Cholesterol	1.84mg
Fibre	3.4g

5 Pour in the remaining stock, add the pasta and bring to the boil, stirring. Reduce the heat and simmer, stirring frequently for 7–8 minutes, or according to the packet instructions, until the pasta is tender or *al dente*. Adjust the seasoning. Remove and discard the rosemary sprig and serve the hot soup in soup bowls, topped with a few rosemary leaves and a little grated Parmesan.

CHICKEN AND PASTA SOUP

—

Skinless cooked chicken, mushrooms and pasta combine well with a flavourful stock, to create
this tasty, low-fat soup, ideal for an appetizer or snack.

3 Remove and discard the skin from the
chicken and slice the meat thinly using a
sharp knife. Add to the soup and season
to taste. Heat the soup through for about
2–3 minutes.

4 Stir in the pasta, bring to the boil, cover
and simmer for 7–8 minutes until tender
or *al dente*. Just before serving, remove
and discard the bay leaf. Stir in the white
wine and chopped parsley, heat through
for 2–3 minutes, then adjust the
seasoning and serve in soup bowls.

INGREDIENTS
900ml/1¹/2 pints/3³/4 cups chicken stock
1 bay leaf
4 spring onions (scallions), sliced
*225g/8oz/3 cups button (white)
mushrooms, sliced*
115g/4oz cooked chicken breast portion
*50g/2oz/¹/2 cup dried soup pasta,
such as stellette*
150ml/¹/4 pint/²/3 cup dry white wine
15ml/1 tbsp chopped fresh parsley
salt and freshly ground black pepper

SERVES 4–6

1 Put the stock and bay leaf into a pan
and bring to the boil.

2 Add the spring onions and mushrooms
and stir to mix.

NUTRITIONAL NOTES
Per portion:

Energy	74Kcals/312kJ
Total fat	1g
Saturated fat	0.3g
Cholesterol	8.24mg
Fibre	0.75g

ROASTED TOMATO AND PASTA SOUP

—

When the only tomatoes you can buy are not particularly flavoursome, make this soup.
The oven-roasting compensates for any lack of flavour in the tomatoes.

INGREDIENTS

*450g/1lb ripe Italian plum tomatoes,
halved lengthways*
*1 large red (bell) pepper, quartered
lengthways and seeded*
1 large red onion, quartered lengthways
2 garlic cloves, unpeeled
15ml/1 tbsp olive oil
*1.2 litres/2 pints/5 cups vegetable stock
or water*
good pinch of sugar
*90g/3¹/₂oz/scant 1 cup dried small pasta
shapes, such as tubetti or small macaroni*
salt and freshly ground black pepper
fresh basil leaves, to garnish

SERVES 4

1 Preheat the oven to 190°C/375°F/Gas 5.
Spread out the tomatoes, red pepper,
onion and garlic in a roasting pan and
drizzle with the olive oil. Roast in the
oven for 30–40 minutes until the
vegetables are soft and charred, stirring
and turning them halfway through the
cooking time.

COOK'S TIP
The soup can be frozen without the
pasta. Thaw and bring to the boil
before adding the pasta.

2 Tip the vegetables into a blender or
food processor, add about 250ml/8fl oz/
1 cup of the stock or water and blend
until puréed. Scrape into a sieve placed
over a large pan and press the purée
through the sieve into the pan. Discard
the contents of the sieve.

3 Add the remaining stock or water, the
sugar and salt and pepper to taste. Bring
to the boil, stirring.

4 Add the pasta and simmer, stirring
frequently, for 7–8 minutes, or according
to the packet instructions, until the
pasta is tender or *al dente*. Adjust the
seasoning. Serve hot in soup bowls,
garnished with fresh basil leaves.

NUTRITIONAL NOTES
Per portion:

Energy	145Kcals/611kJ
Total fat	4.6g
Saturated fat	0.7g
Cholesterol	0mg
Fibre	2.4g

CLAM AND PASTA SOUP

—

This recipe uses store-cupboard (pantry) ingredients to create a delicious and filling low-fat soup. Serve it with hot focaccia or ciabatta for an informal supper with friends.

INGREDIENTS
15ml/1 tbsp olive oil
1 large onion, finely chopped
2 garlic cloves, crushed
400g/14oz can chopped tomatoes
15ml/1 tbsp sun-dried tomato purée (paste)
5ml/1 tsp sugar
5ml/1 tsp dried mixed Italian herbs
about 750ml/1 1/4 pints/3 cups fish or vegetable stock
150ml/1/4 pint/2/3 cup red wine
50g/2oz/1/2 cup small dried pasta shapes
150g/5oz jar or can clams in natural juice
30ml/2 tbsp finely chopped fresh flat leaf parsley, plus a few whole leaves, to garnish
salt and freshly ground black pepper

SERVES 4

1 Heat the oil in a large pan. Cook the onion gently for 5 minutes, stirring frequently, until softened.

NUTRITIONAL NOTES
Per portion:

Energy	165Kcals/695kJ
Total fat	3.4g
Saturated fat	0.4g
Cholesterol	0mg
Fibre	1.5g

2 Add the garlic, tomatoes, tomato purée, sugar, herbs, stock and wine, and salt and pepper to taste. Bring the mixture to the boil. Reduce the heat, half cover the pan and simmer for 10 minutes, stirring the mixture occasionally.

3 Add the pasta and continue simmering, uncovered, for 10 minutes or until the pasta is tender or *al dente*. Stir occasionally.

4 Add the clams and their juice to the soup and heat through for 3–4 minutes, adding more stock if required. Do not let it boil or the clams will be tough. Remove from the heat, stir in the chopped parsley and adjust the seasoning. Serve hot, ladled into soup bowls and sprinkled with coarsely ground black pepper and parsley leaves, to garnish.

CONSOMMÉ WITH AGNOLOTTI

—

A flavourful Italian pasta soup, ideal for a tasty appetizer or snack.

INGREDIENTS

75g/3oz cooked, peeled prawns (shrimp)
75g/3oz canned crab meat, drained
5ml/1 tsp fresh root ginger, peeled and finely grated
15ml/1 tbsp fresh white breadcrumbs
5ml/1 tsp light soy sauce
1 spring onion (scallion), finely chopped
1 garlic clove, crushed
1 quantity of Basic Pasta Dough (see page 14)
egg white, beaten
400g/14oz can chicken or fish consommé
30ml/2 tbsp sherry or vermouth
salt and freshly ground black pepper
50g/2oz cooked, peeled prawns and fresh coriander (cilantro) leaves, to garnish

SERVES 6

1 Put the prawns, crab meat, ginger, breadcrumbs, soy sauce, onion, garlic and seasoning into a blender or food processor and blend until smooth. Set aside.

NUTRITIONAL NOTES

Per portion:

Energy	177Kcals/747kJ
Total fat	2.7g
Saturated fat	0.7g
Cholesterol	89.66mg
Fibre	1g

2 Roll the pasta into thin sheets. Stamp out 32 rounds 5cm/2in in diameter, with a fluted pastry (cookie) cutter.

3 Place a small teaspoon of the puréed filling in the centre of half the pasta rounds. Brush the edges of each round with egg white and sandwich together by placing a second pasta round on top. Pinch the edges together firmly to stop the filling from seeping out.

COOK'S TIP

You can make these pasta shapes a day in advance. Cover and store in the refrigerator.

4 Cook the pasta in a large pan of boiling, salted water for 5 minutes (cook in batches to stop them from sticking together). Remove from the pan and drop into a bowl of cold water for 5 seconds before removing and placing on a tray.

5 Heat the chicken or fish consommé in a pan with the sherry or vermouth. When piping hot, add the cooked pasta shapes and simmer for 1–2 minutes.

6 Serve the cooked pasta in shallow soup bowls covered with hot consommé. Garnish with prawns and coriander.

FARFALLE SALAD WITH PIQUANT PEPPERS

Peppers, pasta and fresh coriander add delicious flavour to this quick and easy
Italian appetizer or supper dish.

INGREDIENTS

1 red, 1 yellow and 1 orange (bell) pepper
1 garlic clove, crushed
30ml/2 tbsp capers
30ml/2 tbsp raisins
5ml/1 tsp wholegrain mustard
finely grated rind and juice of 1 lime
5ml/1 tsp clear honey
30ml/2 tbsp chopped fresh
coriander (cilantro)
225g/8oz/2 cups dried farfalle
salt and freshly ground black pepper
shaved Parmesan cheese, to serve

SERVES 8

1 Quarter the peppers and remove and
discard the stalk and seeds. Put into a
pan of boiling water and cook for about
10–15 minutes until tender. Drain and
rinse under cold water. Drain again. Peel
off and discard the skin and cut the flesh
into strips lengthways. Set aside.

NUTRITIONAL NOTES
Per portion:

Energy	160Kcals/681kJ
Total fat	1g
Saturated fat	0.2g
Cholesterol	0mg
Fibre	1.9g

2 Put the garlic, capers, raisins, mustard,
lime rind and juice, honey, coriander and
seasoning to taste into a bowl and whisk
together. Set aside.

VARIATION
If you prefer, make this salad with only
one colour of pepper. The green ones are
too bitter, however, and are not suitable.

3 Cook the pasta in a large pan of
boiling, salted water for 10–12 minutes
until tender or *al dente*. Drain.

4 Return the pasta to the pan, add the
reserved peppers and dressing. Heat
gently and toss to mix. Transfer to a warm
serving bowl and serve immediately.
Sprinkle with a few shavings of Parmesan
cheese to taste.

CRAB PASTA SALAD WITH SPICY DRESSING

White crab meat and fusilli pasta are tossed together in a spicy dressing to create this flavourful
Italian-style salad which is very low in fat.

INGREDIENTS

350g/12oz/3 cups dried fusilli
1 small red (bell) pepper, seeded and
finely chopped
2 x 175g/6oz cans white crab meat
115g/4oz cherry tomatoes, halved
1/4 cucumber, halved, seeded and sliced
into crescents
15ml/1 tbsp lemon juice
300ml/1/2 pint/11/4 cups low-fat natural
(plain) yogurt
2 celery sticks, finely chopped
10ml/2 tsp horseradish sauce
2.5ml/1/2 tsp ground paprika
2.5ml/1/2 tsp Dijon mustard
30ml/2 tbsp sweet tomato pickle or chutney
salt and freshly ground black pepper
fresh basil, to garnish

SERVES 6

1 Cook the pasta in a large pan of boiling salted water, according to the packet instructions, until tender or *al dente*. Drain and rinse the pasta thoroughly under cold water. Drain again and set aside.

2 Put the red pepper in a bowl and cover with boiling water. Stand for 1 minute. Drain and rinse under cold water. Pat dry on kitchen paper and set aside.

3 Drain the crab meat and pick over carefully. Discard any pieces of shell. Put the crab meat into a bowl with the tomatoes and cucumber. Season with salt and pepper and sprinkle with lemon juice. Set aside.

4 To make the dressing, put the yogurt in a bowl and add the red pepper, celery, horseradish, paprika, mustard and sweet tomato pickle or chutney. Mix the pasta with the crab mixture and dressing and transfer to a serving dish. Garnish with fresh basil and serve.

NUTRITIONAL NOTES
Per portion:

Energy	293Kcals/1244kJ
Total fat	2.3g
Saturated fat	0.5g
Cholesterol	45mg
Fibre	2.4g

SPICY CHICKEN SALAD
—

**This tasty low-fat chicken and pasta salad creates an ideal lunch or
supper dish for family or friends.**

INGREDIENTS

5ml/1 tsp ground cumin seeds
5ml/1 tsp ground paprika
5ml/1 tsp ground turmeric
1–2 garlic cloves, crushed
45–60ml/3–4 tbsp fresh lime juice
*4 small skinless boneless chicken
breast portions*
225g/8oz/2 cups dried rigatoni
1 red (bell) pepper, seeded and chopped
2 celery sticks, thinly sliced
1 shallot or small onion, finely chopped
30 ml/2 tbsp stuffed green olives, halved
30ml/2 tbsp clear honey
10ml/2 tsp wholegrain mustard
salt and freshly ground black pepper
mixed salad leaves, to serve

SERVES 6

1 Mix the cumin, paprika, turmeric,
garlic, seasoning and 30ml/2 tbsp lime
juice in a bowl. Lay the chicken in a
shallow non-metallic dish and rub the
mixture over the chicken breast portions.
Cover with clear film (plastic wrap) and
leave in a cool place for about 3 hours
or overnight.

2 Preheat the oven to 200°C/400°F/Gas 6.
Put the chicken on a grill (broiler) rack in
a single layer and bake in the oven for
20 minutes until cooked. Alternatively,
grill for 8–10 minutes on each side.

3 Meanwhile, cook the rigatoni in a large
pan of boiling, salted water until tender or
al dente. Drain and rinse under cold
water. Leave to drain thoroughly.

4 Put the red pepper, celery, shallot or
onion and olives into a large bowl with
the pasta and toss to mix.

5 Mix the honey, mustard and remaining
lime juice together in a bowl and pour
over the pasta. Toss to mix well.

6 Cut the chicken into bitesize pieces.
Arrange the mixed salad leaves on a
serving dish, spoon the pasta mixture into
the centre of the leaves and top with the
spicy chicken pieces.

NUTRITIONAL NOTES
Per portion:

Energy	234Kcals/993kJ
Total fat	4g
Saturated fat	1.1g
Cholesterol	37.88mg
Fibre	1.6g

DUCK AND PASTA SALAD

Succulent duck breasts are cooked, then sliced and tossed together with pasta and fruit in a delicious virtually fat-free dressing to create this tempting salad.

INGREDIENTS

2 duck breasts, boned
5ml/1 tsp coriander seeds, crushed
350g/12oz dried rigatoni
150ml/1/4 pint/2/3 cup fresh orange juice
15ml/1 tbsp lemon juice
10ml/2 tsp clear honey
1 shallot, finely chopped
1 garlic clove, crushed
1 celery stick, chopped
75g/3oz dried cherries
45ml/3 tbsp port or red wine
15ml/1 tbsp chopped fresh mint, plus extra
to garnish
30ml/2 tbsp chopped fresh coriander
(cilantro), plus extra to garnish
1 eating apple, cored and diced
2 oranges, segmented
salt and freshly ground black pepper

SERVES 6

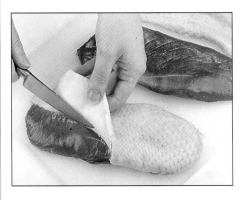

1 Remove and discard the skin and fat from the duck breasts and season with salt and pepper. Rub the duck breasts all over with crushed coriander seeds. Preheat the grill (broiler), then grill (broil) the duck for 7–10 minutes depending on size. Wrap in foil and set aside for about 20 minutes.

2 Meanwhile, cook the pasta in a large pan of boiling, salted water until tender or *al dente*. Drain thoroughly and rinse under cold running water, then drain again. Leave to cool.

3 In the meantime, make the dressing. Put the orange juice, lemon juice, honey, shallot, garlic, celery, cherries, port or red wine, chopped mint and coriander into a bowl, whisk together then set aside for 20–30 minutes.

NUTRITIONAL NOTES
Per portion:

Energy	298Kcals/1266kJ
Total fat	2.3g
Saturated fat	0.5g
Cholesterol	27.5mg
Fibre	3g

4 Slice the duck very thinly. (It should be pink in the centre.)

5 Put the pasta into a bowl, add the duck, dressing, diced apple and segments of orange. Toss well to mix. Transfer the salad to a serving plate and garnish with the extra mint and coriander. Serve.

COOK'S TIP
To skin the duck breasts, slide your fingers between the skin and breast and gently pull to separate. Use a sharp knife to loosen any stubborn parts.

VARIATION
Other shapes of pasta may be substituted for the rigatoni. Penne work well, although long varieties, such as tagliatelle, are also good.

MEAT AND POULTRY PASTA DISHES

Freshly cooked PASTA *topped or tossed with a tasty* LOW-FAT *sauce made with* MEAT *and served with crusty Italian* BREAD *or a salad provides an appealing meal for all to* ENJOY. *Choose from a* VARIETY *of low-fat recipes all packed full of flavour, including low-fat versions of* CLASSIC *dishes such as Spaghetti* BOLOGNESE, *Lasagne and Spaghetti alla* CARBONARA.

SPAGHETTI BOLOGNESE

A very popular Italian dish, this tasty spaghetti Bolognese is full of flavour and is low in fat too.

INGREDIENTS

1 onion, chopped
2–3 garlic cloves, crushed
300ml/¹/2 pint/1¹/4 cups
beef or chicken stock
450g/1lb minced (ground) turkey or beef
2 × 400g/14oz cans chopped tomatoes
5ml/1 tsp dried basil
5ml/1 tsp dried oregano
60ml/4 tbsp tomato purée (paste)
450g/1lb button (white) mushrooms,
quartered and sliced
150ml/¹/4 pint/²/3 cup red wine
450g/1lb dried spaghetti
salt and freshly ground black pepper

SERVES 8

1 Put the chopped onion and garlic into a non-stick pan with half of the stock. Bring to the boil and cook for 5 minutes until the onion is tender and the stock has reduced completely, stirring occasionally.

NUTRITIONAL NOTES
Per portion:

Energy	321Kcals/1350kJ
Total fat	4.1g
Saturated fat	1.3g
Cholesterol	33mg
Fibre	2.7g

2 Add the turkey or beef and cook for 5 minutes, breaking up the meat with a fork. Add the tomatoes, herbs, remaining stock and tomato purée, bring to the boil, then cover, reduce the heat and simmer for 1 hour, stirring occasionally.

COOK'S TIP
Sautéing vegetables in stock rather than oil is an easy way of cutting down calories and fat. Choose fat-free stock to reduce even more.

3 Meanwhile, cook the mushrooms with the wine for 5 minutes in a non-stick pan or until the wine has evaporated, stirring occasionally. Add the mushrooms to the meat, season with salt and pepper to taste and stir to mix.

4 Meanwhile, cook the pasta in a large pan of boiling salted water for 8–12 minutes until tender or *al dente*. Drain thoroughly. Serve the cooked spaghetti topped with the meat sauce.

CHILLI AND PIPE RIGATE

Fresh chilli-flavoured cooked minced meat combines well with pasta to create
a flavourful and filling low-fat supper dish.

INGREDIENTS

450g/1lb minced (ground) beef or turkey
1 onion, finely chopped
2–3 garlic cloves, crushed
1–2 fresh red chillies,
seeded and finely chopped
400g/14oz can chopped tomatoes
45ml/3 tbsp tomato purée (paste)
5ml/1 tsp dried mixed herbs
450g/1lb/4 cups dried pipe rigate
400g/14oz can red kidney beans, drained
salt and freshly ground black pepper

SERVES 6

1 Cook the minced beef or turkey in a
non-stick pan, breaking up any large
pieces with a wooden spoon, until
browned all over.

2 Stir in the onion, garlic and chilli,
cover the pan with a lid and cook gently
for 5 minutes.

3 Stir in the tomatoes, tomato purée,
herbs, 450ml/³/4 pint/scant 2 cups water
and seasoning. Bring to the boil, then
reduce the heat and simmer for 1¹/2 hours,
stirring occasionally. Remove the pan
from the heat and leave to cool slightly.

4 Meanwhile, cook the pasta in a large
pan of boiling, salted water until tender or
al dente. Drain thoroughly. Meanwhile,
skim off and discard any fat from the
surface of the meat. Add the red kidney
beans to the meat and cook for about
5–10 minutes until piping hot, stirring
occasionally. Pour the sauce over the
cooked pasta and serve.

NUTRITIONAL NOTES

Per portion:

Energy	246Kcals/1042kJ
Total fat	1.8g
Saturated fat	0.4g
Cholesterol	38.5mg
Fibre	6g

SPAGHETTI WITH MEATBALLS

Italian-style meatballs simmered in a sweet and spicy tomato sauce are truly delicious served
with spaghetti, making an ideal low-fat dish for all the family to enjoy.

INGREDIENTS
350g/12oz minced (ground) beef
1 egg
*60ml/4 tbsp coarsely chopped fresh
flat leaf parsley*
2.5ml/1/2 tsp crushed dried red chillies
1 thick slice white bread, crusts removed
30ml/2 tbsp semi-skimmed (low-fat) milk
15ml/1 tbsp olive oil
*300ml/1/2 pint/11/4 cups passata (bottled
strained tomatoes)*
400ml/14fl oz/12/3 cups vegetable stock
5ml/1 tsp sugar
450g/1lb dried spaghetti
salt and freshly ground black pepper
*40g/11/2oz/1/2 cup grated fresh Parmesan
cheese, to serve*

SERVES 8

1 Put the beef in a bowl. Add the egg,
half the parsley and half the chillies.
Season with salt and pepper. Mix well.

2 Tear the bread into small pieces and
place in a small bowl. Moisten with the
milk. Leave to soak for a few minutes,
then squeeze out and discard the excess
milk and crumble the bread over the meat
mixture. Mix everything together with a
wooden spoon, then use your hands to
squeeze and knead the mixture so that it
becomes smooth and quite sticky.

3 Wash your hands, rinse them under
cold water, then pick up small pieces of
the mixture and roll them between your
palms to make about 40–60 small balls.

4 Place the meatballs on a tray and chill
in the refrigerator for about 30 minutes.

5 Heat the oil in a large non-stick frying
pan. Cook the meatballs, in batches, until
browned all over. Set aside.

6 Pour the passata and stock into a large
pan. Heat gently, then add the remaining
chillies and the sugar, with salt and
pepper to taste. Add the meatballs to the
passata mixture, then bring to the boil.
Reduce the heat, cover and simmer for
20 minutes, stirring occasionally.

7 Cook the pasta in a large pan of boiling
salted water, according to the packet
instructions until it is tender or
al dente. Drain well and tip it into a
warmed large bowl. Pour the sauce over
the pasta and toss gently to mix. Sprinkle
with the remaining parsley and serve with
grated Parmesan handed separately.

NUTRITIONAL NOTES
Per portion:

Energy	148Kcals/622kJ
Total fat	5g
Saturated fat	1.9g
Cholesterol	44.8mg
Fibre	0.9g

SPAGHETTI WITH SPICY BEEF SAUCE

This is a delicious spicy version of spaghetti Bolognese, which is not an authentic Italian dish.
It was "invented" by Italian émigrés in America in the 1960s in response to popular demand.

INGREDIENTS
10ml/2 tsp olive oil
1 onion, finely chopped
1 garlic clove, crushed
5ml/1 tsp dried mixed herbs
1.5ml/¼ tsp cayenne pepper
450g/1lb minced (ground) beef
400g/14oz can chopped
Italian plum tomatoes
45ml/3 tbsp tomato ketchup
15ml/1 tbsp sun-dried tomato
purée (paste)
5ml/1 tsp Worcestershire sauce
5ml/1 tsp dried oregano
450ml/¾ pint/scant 2 cups beef
or vegetable stock
45ml/3 tbsp red wine
450g/1lb dried spaghetti
salt and freshly ground black pepper
25g/1oz/⅓ cup grated fresh Parmesan
cheese, to serve (optional)

SERVES 6

1 Heat the oil in a medium pan, add the onion and garlic and cook over a low heat, stirring frequently, for about 5 minutes until softened. Stir in the mixed herbs and cayenne and cook for a further 2–3 minutes. Add the minced beef and cook gently for about 5 minutes, stirring frequently and breaking up any lumps in the meat with a wooden spoon.

2 Stir in the tomatoes, tomato ketchup, sun-dried tomato purée, Worcestershire sauce, oregano and plenty of ground black pepper. Pour in the stock and red wine and bring to the boil, stirring constantly. Cover the pan, reduce the heat and simmer the sauce for 30 minutes, stirring occasionally.

3 Meanwhile, cook the pasta in a large pan of boiling salted water, according to the packet instructions, until tender or *al dente*. Drain, and divide among warmed bowls. Taste the meat sauce and add a little salt if necessary, then spoon it on top of the pasta and sprinkle with a little grated Parmesan, if using. Serve immediately.

NUTRITIONAL NOTES
Per portion:

Energy	207Kcals/874kJ
Total fat	4.9g
Saturated fat	1.5g
Cholesterol	39.1mg
Fibre	1.8g

LASAGNE

—

This is a delicious low-fat version of the classic Italian lasagne, ideal served with a mixed salad
and crusty bread for an appetizing supper with friends.

INGREDIENTS

1 large onion, chopped
2 garlic cloves, crushed
500g/1¼lb extra-lean minced (ground)
beef or turkey
450g/1lb passata (bottled
strained tomatoes)
5ml/1 tsp dried mixed herbs
225g/8oz frozen leaf spinach, thawed
200g/7oz lasagne verdi
200g/7oz/scant 1 cup cottage cheese

FOR THE SAUCE

25g/1oz low-fat spread
25g/1oz/¼ cup plain (all-purpose) flour
300ml/½ pint/1¼ cups skimmed milk
1.5ml/¼ tsp ground nutmeg
25g/1oz/⅓ cup grated Parmesan cheese
salt and freshly ground black pepper

SERVES 8

1 Put the onion, garlic and minced meat
into a non-stick pan. Cook quickly for
5 minutes, stirring with a wooden spoon
to separate the pieces, until the meat is
lightly browned all over.

COOK'S TIP

Make sure you use the type of lasagne
that does not require any pre-cooking
for this recipe.

2 Add the passata, herbs and seasoning
and stir to mix. Bring to the boil, cover,
then reduce the heat and simmer for
about 30 minutes, stirring occasionally.

3 Make the sauce: put all the sauce
ingredients, except the Parmesan
cheese, into a pan. Cook until the sauce
thickens, whisking constantly until
bubbling and smooth. Turn the heat off.
Adjust the seasoning to taste, add
the Parmesan cheese to the sauce and
stir to mix.

NUTRITIONAL NOTES

Per portion:

Energy	244Kcals/1032kJ
Total fat	4.8g
Saturated fat	1.9g
Cholesterol	37.9mg
Fibre	2g

4 Preheat the oven to 190°C/375°F/Gas 5.
Lay the spinach leaves out on sheets of
absorbent kitchen paper and pat them
until they are dry.

5 Layer the meat mixture, lasagne,
cottage cheese and spinach leaves in a
2 litre/3½ pint/8 cup ovenproof dish,
starting and ending with a layer of meat.

6 Spoon the sauce over the top to cover
the meat completely and bake in the oven
for 40–50 minutes or until bubbling.
Serve immediately.

TAGLIATELLE WITH MEAT SAUCE

This recipe is an authentic meat sauce – ragù – from the city of Bologna in Emilia-Romagna. It is
quite rich and very delicious, and is always served with tagliatelle, never with spaghetti.

INGREDIENTS
450g/1lb dried tagliatelle
salt and freshly ground black pepper
grated fresh Parmesan cheese,
to serve (optional)

FOR THE BOLOGNESE MEAT SAUCE
1 onion
2 carrots
2 celery sticks
2 garlic cloves
15ml/1 tbsp olive oil
115g/4oz lean bacon, diced
250g/9oz extra-lean minced (ground) beef
250g/9oz extra-lean minced (ground) pork
120ml/4fl oz/1/2 cup dry white wine
2 × 400g/14oz cans crushed
Italian plum tomatoes
475–750ml/16fl oz–11/4 pints/2–3 cups
beef stock

SERVES 8

1 Make the meat sauce. Chop all the
fresh vegetables finely. Heat the oil in a
large pan or frying pan. Add the chopped
vegetables and the bacon and cook over
a medium heat, stirring frequently, for
about 10 minutes or until the vegetables
have softened.

2 Add the minced beef and pork, reduce
the heat and cook gently for 10 minutes,
stirring frequently and breaking up any
lumps in the meat with a wooden spoon.

3 Stir in salt and pepper to taste, then
add the wine and stir again. Simmer for
about 5 minutes, or until reduced.

4 Add the tomatoes and 250ml/8fl oz/
1 cup of the stock and bring to the boil.
Stir the sauce well, then reduce the heat.
Half cover the pan with a lid and simmer
very gently for 2 hours. Stir the sauce
occasionally and add more stock as it
becomes absorbed.

5 Simmer the sauce, without a lid, for a
further 30 minutes, stirring frequently.
Meanwhile, cook the pasta in a large pan
of boiling salted water, according to the
packet instructions, until tender or *al
dente*. Taste the sauce and adjust the
seasoning. Drain the cooked pasta and tip
it into a warmed bowl. Pour the meat
sauce over the pasta and toss well. Serve
immediately, sprinkled with grated
Parmesan, if using.

NUTRITIONAL NOTES
Per portion:

Energy	185Kcals/782kJ
Total fat	5g
Saturated fat	1.7g
Cholesterol	36.3mg
Fibre	1.8g

LAMB AND SWEET PEPPER SAUCE

This simple sauce is a speciality of the Abruzzo-Molise region of Italy, east of Rome, where it is traditionally served with *maccheroni alla chitarra* – square-shaped long macaroni.

2 Sprinkle in the garlic and add the bay leaves, then pour in the wine and let it bubble until reduced.

3 Add the tomatoes and peppers and stir to mix. Season again. Cover with a lid, bring to the boil, then reduce the heat and simmer gently for 45–55 minutes or until the lamb is very tender. Stir occasionally during cooking and add a little water if the sauce becomes too dry. Meanwhile, cook the pasta in a large pan of boiling salted water, according to the packet instructions, until tender or *al dente*. Drain well. Remove and discard the bay leaves from the lamb sauce before serving it with the cooked pasta.

INGREDIENTS

15ml/1 tbsp olive oil
250g/9oz boneless lean lamb neck (shoulder) fillet, diced quite small
2 garlic cloves, finely chopped
2 bay leaves, torn
250ml/8fl oz/1 cup dry white wine
4 ripe Italian plum tomatoes, peeled and chopped
2 red (bell) peppers, seeded and diced
450g/1lb dried spaghetti
salt and freshly ground black pepper

SERVES 6

1 Heat the oil in a medium frying pan or pan, add the lamb and a little salt and pepper. Cook over a medium to high heat for about 10 minutes, stirring frequently, until browned all over.

NUTRITIONAL NOTES

Per portion:

Energy	179Kcals/755kJ
Total fat	5g
Saturated fat	1.8g
Cholesterol	28mg
Fibre	1.4g

COOK'S TIP

You can make your own fresh *maccheroni alla chitarra* or buy the dried pasta from an Italian delicatessen. Alternatively, this sauce is just as good served with ordinary spaghetti or long or short macaroni.

VARIATION

The peppers don't have to be red. Use yellow, orange or green if you like; either one colour or a mixture.

TAGLIOLINI WITH MEATY TOMATO SAUCE

—

Serve cooked tagliolini or tagliarini with this delicious meat-flavoured tomato sauce for an appetizing main course or supper.

INGREDIENTS

1 small onion

1 small carrot

2 celery sticks

2 garlic cloves

1 small handful of fresh flat leaf parsley

50g/2oz lean ham or bacon, finely chopped

60–90ml/4–6 tbsp dry white wine,

or more to taste

500g/1¼lb ripe Italian plum

tomatoes, chopped

350g/12oz dried tagliolini or tagliarini

salt and freshly ground black pepper

fresh flat leaf parsley sprigs, to garnish

SERVES 4

1 Chop the onion, carrot and celery finely in a food processor. Add the garlic cloves and parsley and process until finely chopped. Alternatively, chop everything by hand.

2 Put the chopped vegetable mixture in a medium shallow pan or frying pan with the ham or bacon and cook, stirring, over a low heat for about 5 minutes. Add the wine, with salt and pepper to taste, and simmer for 5 minutes, then stir in the tomatoes. Bring to the boil, reduce the heat and simmer for 40 minutes, stirring occasionally and adding a little hot water if the sauce seems too dry.

3 Have ready a large sieve placed over a large bowl. Carefully pour in the sauce and press it through the sieve with the back of a metal spoon, leaving behind the tomato skins and any tough pieces of vegetable that won't go through. Discard the contents of the sieve.

4 Return the sauce to the rinsed-out pan and heat it through, adding a little more wine or hot water if it is too thick. Taste the sauce and adjust the seasoning if necessary. Meanwhile, cook the pasta in a large pan of boiling salted water, according to the packet instructions, until tender or *al dente*. Drain thoroughly. Toss the cooked pasta with the tomato sauce and serve immediately, garnished with fresh parsley sprigs.

NUTRITIONAL NOTES

Per portion:

Energy	187Kcals/790kJ
Total fat	3.3g
Saturated fat	1g
Cholesterol	8.8mg
Fibre	2.7g

RIGATONI WITH PORK

This is an excellent and very tasty, low-fat meat sauce made using lean pork rather than the more usual beef. You could serve it with tagliatelle or spaghetti instead of rigatoni.

INGREDIENTS

1 small onion
1/2 carrot
1/2 celery stick
2 garlic cloves
15ml/1 tbsp olive oil
150g/5oz extra-lean minced (ground) pork
60ml/4 tbsp dry white wine
400g/14oz can chopped Italian plum tomatoes
a few fresh basil leaves, plus extra basil leaves, to garnish
400g/14oz/3 1/2 cups dried rigatoni
salt and freshly ground black pepper
freshly shaved Parmesan cheese, to serve (optional)

SERVES 4

1 Chop the fresh vegetables and garlic finely, in a food processor or by hand. Heat the oil in a large frying pan or pan until just sizzling, add the vegetables and cook over a medium heat, stirring frequently, for 3–4 minutes.

VARIATION
To give the sauce a more intense flavour, soak 15g/1/2oz/1/4 cup dried porcini mushrooms in 175ml/6fl oz/3/4 cup warm water for 15–20 minutes, then drain, chop and add them with the meat.

2 Add the pork and cook gently for 2–3 minutes, breaking up any lumps in the meat with a wooden spoon.

3 Reduce the heat and cook for a further 2–3 minutes, stirring frequently, then stir in the wine. Mix in the tomatoes, whole basil leaves, salt to taste and plenty of pepper. Bring to the boil, then reduce the heat, cover and simmer for 40 minutes, stirring occasionally.

4 Cook the pasta in a large pan of boiling salted water, according to the packet instructions, until tender or *al dente*. Just before draining it, add a ladleful or two of the cooking water to the sauce. Stir well, then taste the sauce and adjust the seasoning if necessary.

5 Drain the pasta, add it to the pan of sauce and toss well. Serve immediately, sprinkled with the basil leaves and shaved Parmesan, if using.

NUTRITIONAL NOTES
Per portion:

Energy	70Kcals/293kJ
Total fat	2.5g
Saturated fat	0.4g
Cholesterol	0mg
Fibre	2.4g

TAGLIATELLE WITH MILANESE SAUCE

Tagliatelle is served with a tasty, low-fat version of the classic Milanese sauce to create this flavourful dish, ideal for a family meal.

INGREDIENTS

1 onion, finely chopped
1 celery stick, finely chopped
1 red (bell) pepper, seeded
and diced
1–2 garlic cloves, crushed
150ml/1/4 pint/2/3 cup vegetable
or chicken stock
400g/14oz can tomatoes
15ml/1 tbsp tomato purée (paste)
10ml/2 tsp caster (superfine) sugar
5ml/1 tsp dried
mixed herbs
350g/12oz tagliatelle
115g/4oz button (white) or small cap
mushrooms, sliced
60ml/4 tbsp dry white wine
115g/4oz lean cooked ham,
coarsely diced
salt and freshly ground black pepper
15ml/1 tbsp chopped fresh parsley,
to garnish

SERVES 4

1 Put the onion, celery, red pepper and garlic into a pan.

2 Add the stock, bring to the boil and cook for 5 minutes or until tender, stirring occasionally.

3 Add the tomatoes, tomato purée, sugar and dried herbs. Season with salt and pepper.

4 Bring to the boil, then reduce the heat and simmer for 30 minutes, stirring occasionally, until the sauce is thick.

5 Cook the pasta in a large pan of boiling salted water, according to the packet instructions, until tender or *al dente*. Drain thoroughly.

6 Meanwhile, put the mushrooms into a small pan with the white wine, cover and cook for 3–4 minutes until the mushrooms are tender and all the wine has been absorbed, stirring occasionally.

7 Stir the mushrooms and ham into the tomato sauce and reheat gently over a low heat until piping hot.

8 Transfer the pasta to a warmed serving dish and spoon the sauce on top. Garnish with chopped parsley and serve.

NUTRITIONAL NOTES
Per portion:

Energy	405Kcals/1700kJ
Total fat	3.5g
Saturated fat	0.8g
Cholesterol	17mg
Fibre	4.5g

COOK'S TIP
To reduce the calorie and fat content even more, omit the ham and use sweetcorn kernels or cooked broccoli florets instead.

SPAGHETTI ALLA CARBONARA

This is a low-fat variation of the classic Italian charcoal burner's spaghetti, using lean smoked bacon and low-fat cream cheese. Serve with a few Parmesan cheese shavings.

2 Add the wine and boil rapidly until reduced by half. Whisk in the cheese and season to taste with salt and pepper.

3 Meanwhile, cook the spaghetti in a large pan of boiling, salted water for 10–12 minutes, until tender or *al dente*. Drain thoroughly.

4 Return the cooked spaghetti to the pan with the sauce and parsley, toss well and serve immediately topped with a few thin shavings of Parmesan cheese.

INGREDIENTS
150g/5oz smoked bacon rashers (strips)
1 onion, chopped
1–2 garlic cloves, crushed
150ml/¼ pint/⅔ cup chicken stock
150ml/¼ pint/⅔ cup dry white wine
200g/7oz/scant 1 cup low-fat soft cheese
450g/1lb chilli and garlic-flavoured dried spaghetti
30ml/2 tbsp chopped fresh parsley
salt and freshly ground black pepper
15g/½oz shaved fresh Parmesan cheese, to serve

SERVES 4

1 Cut the bacon rashers into 1cm/½in strips. Fry quickly in a non-stick frying pan for 2–3 minutes, stirring. Add the onion, garlic and stock to the pan. Bring to the boil, cover, then reduce the heat and simmer for about 5 minutes until tender.

NUTRITIONAL NOTES
Per portion:

Energy	428Kcals/1815kJ
Total fat	4.6g
Saturated fat	1.6g
Cholesterol	9.96mg
Fibre	3g

PAPPARDELLE WITH RABBIT SAUCE

—

This delicious low-fat pasta dish comes from the north of Italy, where rabbit sauces for pasta
are very popular. Serve with crusty fresh bread and a mixed leaf salad for a filling meal.

INGREDIENTS

15g/¹/₂oz/¹/₄ cup dried porcini mushrooms
175ml/6fl oz/³/₄ cup warm water
1 small onion
¹/₂ carrot
¹/₂ celery stick
2 bay leaves
15ml/1 tbsp olive oil
40g/1¹/₂oz lean back bacon, chopped
*15ml/1 tbsp roughly chopped fresh flat leaf
parsley, plus extra to garnish*
350g/12oz boneless lean rabbit meat
90ml/6 tbsp dry white wine
*200g/7oz can chopped Italian plum
tomatoes or 200ml/7fl oz/scant
1 cup passata (bottled strained tomatoes)*
450g/1lb dried pappardelle
salt and freshly ground black pepper

SERVES 6

1 Put the dried mushrooms in a bowl,
pour over the warm water and leave to
soak for 15–20 minutes. Finely chop the
fresh vegetables. Make a tear in each bay
leaf, so they release their flavour.

2 Heat the oil in a frying pan or medium
pan. Add the vegetables, bacon and
parsley and cook for about 5 minutes,
stirring occasionally.

NUTRITIONAL NOTES

Per portion:

Energy	166Kcals/699kJ
Total fat	4.7g
Saturated fat	1.4g
Cholesterol	33.9mg
Fibre	1.4g

3 Add the pieces of rabbit and fry on both
sides for 3–4 minutes, stirring frequently.
Pour the wine over and let it bubble and
reduce for a few minutes, then add the
tomatoes or passata. Drain the soaked
mushrooms and pour the soaking liquid
into the pan. Chop the mushrooms and
add them to the pan with the bay leaves
and salt and pepper to taste. Stir well,
cover, bring to the boil, then reduce the
heat and simmer for 35–40 minutes until
the rabbit is tender, stirring occasionally.

4 Remove from the heat and lift out the
rabbit with a slotted spoon. Cut into
bitesize chunks and stir into the sauce.
Remove the bay leaves. Add more salt
and pepper, if needed. Cook the pasta in
a large pan of boiling salted water,
according to the packet instructions,
until tender or *al dente*. Meanwhile,
reheat the sauce until piping hot. Drain
the pasta and toss with the sauce in a
warmed bowl. Serve immediately,
sprinkled with parsley.

FISH AND SHELLFISH PASTA DISHES

The wide variety of different SHAPES, sizes and flavours of FRESH and dried pasta creates a wonderful basis for many delicious and NUTRITIOUS low-fat fish and shellfish PASTA dishes. We include a tempting selection of no-fuss recipes, using a variety of FISH and SHELLFISH, to please every palate. Choose from Farfalle with TUNA, Smoked Trout Cannelloni, Tagliatelle with Scallops or Spaghetti with CLAM Sauce.

SPAGHETTI WITH TUNA SAUCE

A speedy low-fat midweek meal, which can also be made with other pasta shapes, this tasty Italian pasta dish is ideal for all the family.

INGREDIENTS

225g/8oz dried spaghetti, or 450g/1lb fresh
1 garlic clove, crushed
400g/14oz can chopped tomatoes
425g/15oz can tuna in brine, drained and flaked
2.5ml/¹/₂ tsp chilli sauce (optional)
4 pitted black olives, chopped
salt and freshly ground black pepper

SERVES 4

2 Add the garlic and tomatoes to the pan and bring to the boil. Simmer gently, uncovered, for 2–3 minutes, stirring the mixture occasionally.

3 Add the tuna, chilli sauce, if using, the olives and spaghetti. Heat gently until hot, stirring constantly. Add seasoning to taste and serve hot.

1 Cook the spaghetti in a large pan of boiling salted water for 12 minutes or until just tender or *al dente*. Drain well and keep hot.

COOK'S TIP

If fresh tuna is available, use 450g/1lb, cut into small chunks, and add after Step 2. Simmer for 6–8 minutes, then add the chilli, olives and pasta.

NUTRITIONAL NOTES

Per portion:

Energy	306Kcals/1288kJ
Total fat	2.02g
Saturated fat	0.37g
Cholesterol	48.45mg
Fibre	2.46g

PASTA WITH TOMATO AND TUNA

—

Pasta shells are topped with a tasty tuna and tomato sauce to create this delicious,
low-fat Italian-style pasta dish.

3 Meanwhile, cook the pasta in a large pan of boiling, salted water according to the packet instructions, until tender or *al dente*. Drain thoroughly and transfer to a warm serving dish.

4 With a fork, flake the tuna into large chunks and add to the sauce with the capers. Cook gently for 1–2 minutes, stirring constantly, then pour over the pasta, toss gently and serve immediately.

INGREDIENTS

1 onion, finely chopped
1 celery stick, finely chopped
1 red (bell) pepper, seeded and diced
1 garlic clove, crushed
150ml/¼ pint/⅔ cup chicken stock
400g/14oz can chopped tomatoes
15ml/1 tbsp tomato purée (paste)
10ml/2 tsp caster (superfine) sugar
15ml/1 tbsp chopped fresh basil
15ml/1 tbsp chopped fresh parsley
450g/1lb/4 cups dried conchiglie
400g/14oz can tuna in brine, drained
30ml/2 tbsp capers in vinegar, drained
salt and freshly ground black pepper

SERVES 6

1 Put the onion, celery, red pepper and garlic into a pan. Add the stock, bring to the boil and cook for 5 minutes until the stock has reduced significantly.

2 Add the tomatoes, tomato purée, sugar and herbs. Season to taste with salt and pepper and bring to the boil. Reduce the heat and simmer for about 30 minutes until thick, stirring occasionally.

VARIATION

If fresh herbs are not available, use a 400g/14oz can of chopped tomatoes with herbs and add 5–10ml/1–2 tsp dried mixed herbs, in place of the fresh herbs.

NUTRITIONAL NOTES

Per portion:

Energy	369Kcals/1549kJ
Total fat	2.1g
Saturated fat	0.4g
Cholesterol	34mg
Fibre	4g

FARFALLE WITH TUNA

—

This is a quick and simple dish that makes a good low-fat weekday supper if you have canned tomatoes and tuna to hand. Serve with crusty fresh Italian bread.

4 Meanwhile, cook the pasta in a large pan of boiling salted water according to the packet instructions, until tender or *al dente*.

5 Drain the tuna and flake it with a fork. Add to the sauce with about 60ml/4 tbsp of the pasta water and stir to mix. Adjust the seasoning to taste.

6 Drain the pasta well and tip it into a warmed serving bowl. Pour the sauce over the top and toss to mix. Serve immediately, garnished with oregano.

INGREDIENTS

15ml/1 tbsp olive oil
1 small onion, finely chopped
1 garlic clove, finely chopped
400g/14oz can chopped Italian plum tomatoes
45ml/3 tbsp dry white wine
8–10 pitted black olives, sliced into rings
10ml/2 tsp chopped fresh oregano or 5ml/1 tsp dried oregano, plus extra fresh oregano, to garnish
350g/12oz/3 cups dried farfalle
175g/6oz can tuna in brine
salt and freshly ground black pepper

SERVES 4

1 Heat the olive oil over a low heat in a medium frying pan, and add the chopped onion and garlic.

2 Cook gently, stirring occasionally, for 2–3 minutes until the onion is soft and golden brown.

3 Add the tomatoes and bring to the boil, then add the white wine and simmer for a minute or so. Stir in the olives and oregano, with salt and pepper to taste, then cover and cook for 20–25 minutes, stirring occasionally.

NUTRITIONAL NOTES
Per portion:

Energy	387Kcals/1643kJ
Total fat	4.9g
Saturated fat	0.8g
Cholesterol	21.3mg
Fibre	3.5g

MACARONI WITH BROCCOLI AND CAULIFLOWER

—

This is a typical southern Italian dish, full of flavour and low in fat too. Without the anchovies, it can be served to vegetarians.

INGREDIENTS

*175g/6oz cauliflower florets, cut into
small sprigs
175g/6oz broccoli florets, cut into
small sprigs
350g/12oz/3 cups dried
short-cut macaroni
15ml/1 tbsp extra virgin olive oil
1 onion, finely chopped
30ml/2 tbsp pine nuts (optional)
1 sachet of saffron powder, dissolved in
15ml/1 tbsp warm water
15ml/1 tbsp raisins
30ml/2 tbsp sun-dried tomato purée (paste)
4 bottled or canned anchovies in olive oil,
drained and chopped
salt and freshly ground black pepper
grated fresh Pecorino cheese,
to serve (optional)*

SERVES 4

3 Meanwhile, heat the olive oil in a large frying pan, add the onion and cook over a low to medium heat, stirring frequently, for 2–3 minutes or until golden. Add the pine nuts, if using, the broccoli and cauliflower, and the saffron water. Add the raisins, sun-dried tomato purée and a couple of ladlefuls of the pasta cooking water and stir in until the mixture has the consistency of a sauce. Finally, season with plenty of pepper.

4 Stir well, cook for 1–2 minutes, then add the chopped anchovies. Drain the pasta and tip it into the vegetable mixture. Toss well, then taste for seasoning and add salt if necessary. Serve the pasta immediately in 4 warmed bowls, sprinkled with freshly grated Pecorino, if using.

NUTRITIONAL NOTES

Per portion:

Energy	339Kcals/1438kJ
Total fat	5g
Saturated fat	0.7g
Cholesterol	0mg
Fibre	4.5g

1 Cook the cauliflower in a large pan of boiling salted water for 3 minutes. Add the broccoli and boil for a further 2 minutes. Remove the vegetables from the pan with a large slotted spoon, place on a plate and set aside.

2 Add the pasta to the vegetable cooking water and bring back to the boil. Cook the pasta according to the packet instructions, until it is tender or *al dente*.

SMOKED TROUT CANNELLONI

—

Cannelloni are stuffed with a tasty smoked trout filling, topped with a low-fat cheese sauce and oven-baked to create this appetizing lunch or supper dish.

INGREDIENTS

1 large onion, finely chopped
1 garlic clove, crushed
60ml/4 tbsp vegetable stock
2 × 400g/14oz cans chopped tomatoes
2.5ml/1/2 tsp dried mixed herbs
1 smoked trout, weighing about 400g/14oz
75g/3oz/3/4 cup frozen peas, thawed
75g/3oz/11/2 cups fresh breadcrumbs
16 cannelloni tubes
salt and freshly ground black pepper
mixed salad, to serve

FOR THE CHEESE SAUCE

25g/1oz/2 tbsp low-fat spread
25g/1oz/1/4 cup plain (all-purpose) flour
350ml/12fl oz/11/2 cups skimmed milk
freshly grated nutmeg
15g/1/2oz/11/2 tbsp finely grated fresh
Parmesan cheese

SERVES 6

1 Simmer the onion, garlic and stock in a large covered pan for 3 minutes. Uncover the pan and continue to cook, stirring occasionally, until reduced entirely.

COOK'S TIP

Smoked trout can be bought already filleted or whole. If you buy fillets, you'll need 225g/8oz fish.

2 Stir in the tomatoes and herbs. Simmer uncovered for a further 10 minutes, or until very thick, stirring occasionally.

3 Meanwhile, skin the smoked trout with a sharp knife. Carefully flake the flesh and discard all the bones. Mix with the tomato mixture, peas, breadcrumbs, salt and pepper in a large bowl.

4 Preheat the oven to 190°C/375°F/Gas 5. Spoon the filling into the cannelloni tubes and arrange in an ovenproof dish. Set aside.

5 Make the sauce. Put the low-fat spread, flour and milk into a pan and cook over a medium heat, whisking until the sauce thickens. Simmer for 2–3 minutes, stirring constantly. Season to taste with salt, pepper and nutmeg.

6 Pour the sauce over the cannelloni and sprinkle with the Parmesan cheese. Bake in the oven for 35–40 minutes, or until the top is golden brown. Serve with a mixed salad.

NUTRITIONAL NOTES

Per portion:

Energy	306Kcals/1298kJ
Total fat	5g
Saturated fat	1.3g
Cholesterol	45.8mg
Fibre	3g

FUSILLI WITH SMOKED TROUT

—

Fusilli pasta is served with a delicious smoked trout and vegetable sauce to create a flavourful
lunch or supper dish. Smoked salmon may be used in place of the trout, for a tasty change.

INGREDIENTS

2 carrots, cut into julienne sticks
1 leek, cut into julienne sticks
2 celery sticks, cut into
julienne sticks
150ml/¹/4 pint/²/3 cup vegetable or
fish stock
225g/8oz smoked trout fillets,
skinned and cut into strips
200g/7oz/scant 1 cup low-fat soft cheese
150ml/¹/4 pint/²/3 cup medium sweet
white wine or fish stock
15ml/1 tbsp chopped fresh dill or fennel
225g/8oz dried fusilli lunghi
salt and freshly ground black pepper
fresh dill sprigs, to garnish

SERVES 6

1 Put the carrots, leek and celery into
a pan with the vegetable or fish stock.
Bring to the boil and cook quickly for
4–5 minutes until the vegetables are
tender and most of the stock has
evaporated, stirring occasionally. Turn
the heat off and stir in the smoked trout.
Set aside.

2 To make the sauce, put the soft cheese
and wine or fish stock into a pan and
cook, whisking until smooth. Season. Stir
in the dill or fennel.

3 Meanwhile, cook the pasta in a large
pan of boiling salted water according to
the instructions, until tender or *al dente*.
Drain thoroughly. Return to the pan, add
the sauce, toss and transfer to a serving
bowl. Top with the vegetables and trout.
Serve garnished with dill sprigs.

NUTRITIONAL NOTES
Per portion:

Energy	234Kcals/989kJ
Total fat	3.7g
Saturated fat	1.3g
Cholesterol	40mg
Fibre	1.7g

BLACK TAGLIATELLE WITH CREAMY SCALLOPS

—

Low-fat fromage frais (sour cream), cooked with mustard, garlic, herbs and scallops, makes this deceptively creamy and delicious sauce ideal for serving with cooked pasta for a flavourful meal.

INGREDIENTS

120ml/4fl oz/¹/2 cup low-fat fromage frais
10ml/2 tsp wholegrain mustard
2 garlic cloves, crushed
30–45ml/2–3 tbsp fresh lime juice
60ml/4 tbsp chopped fresh parsley
30ml/2 tbsp chopped fresh chives
350g/12oz dried black tagliatelle
12 large fresh scallops
60ml/4 tbsp white wine
150ml/¹/4 pint/²/3 cup fish stock
salt and freshly ground black pepper
lime wedges and fresh parsley sprigs,
to garnish

SERVES 4

1 To make the sauce, mix the fromage frais (sour cream), mustard, garlic, lime juice, chopped parsley, chives and seasoning together in a mixing bowl. Set aside.

NUTRITIONAL NOTES
Per portion:

Energy	368Kcals/1561kJ
Total fat	4.01g
Saturated fat	0.98g
Cholesterol	99mg
Fibre	1.91g

2 Cook the pasta in a large pan of boiling salted water according to the packet instructions, until tender or *al dente*. Drain thoroughly and keep hot.

3 Slice the scallops in half horizontally. Keep any coral whole. Put the wine and fish stock into a pan and heat to simmering point. Add the scallops and cook very gently for 3–4 minutes (but not for any longer or they will toughen).

4 Remove the scallops, place on a plate and keep warm. Boil the wine and stock to reduce by half and then add the green sauce to the pan. Heat gently to warm through, stirring, then return the scallops to the pan and cook for 1 minute. Spoon the sauce over the cooked pasta and garnish with lime wedges and fresh parsley sprigs. Serve immediately.

TAGLIATELLE WITH SCALLOPS

—

Scallops and brandy add a taste of luxury to this appetizing pasta sauce, ideal as a supper dish.

INGREDIENTS
200g/7oz scallops, sliced
30ml/2 tbsp plain (all-purpose) flour
15ml/1 tbsp olive oil
2 spring onions (scallions), cut into thin rings
1/2–1 small fresh red chilli, seeded and very finely chopped
30ml/2 tbsp finely chopped fresh flat leaf parsley
60ml/4 tbsp brandy
105ml/7 tbsp fish stock
275g/10oz fresh spinach-flavoured tagliatelle
salt and freshly ground black pepper

SERVES 4

1 Toss the scallops in the flour, shaking off the excess. Bring a large pan of salted water to the boil for the pasta. Meanwhile, heat the olive oil in a frying pan. Add the spring onions, chilli and half the parsley and cook, stirring frequently, for 1–2 minutes over a medium heat. Add the scallops and toss for 1–2 minutes.

2 Pour the brandy over the scallops, then set it alight. When the flames have died down, pour in the stock, season to taste with salt and pepper and stir. Simmer for 2–3 minutes, then cover and remove from the heat. Cook the pasta according to the packet instructions. Drain, add to the sauce and toss over a medium heat until mixed. Serve immediately.

NUTRITIONAL NOTES
Per portion:

Energy	372Kcals/1576kJ
Total fat	4.8g
Saturated fat	0.7g
Cholesterol	0.0mg
Fibre	2.2g

SPAGHETTI WITH SQUID AND PEAS

—

In Tuscany, squid is often cooked with peas in a tomato sauce. This low-fat recipe is a tasty variation on the theme, and it works very well.

INGREDIENTS
450g/1lb prepared squid
10ml/2 tsp olive oil
1 small onion, finely chopped
400g/14oz can chopped Italian plum tomatoes
1 garlic clove, finely chopped
15ml/1 tbsp red wine vinegar
5ml/1 tsp sugar
10ml/2 tsp finely chopped fresh rosemary
115g/4oz/1 cup frozen peas
275g/10oz dried spaghetti
15ml/1 tbsp chopped fresh flat leaf parsley
salt and freshly ground black pepper

SERVES 4

1 Cut the prepared squid into strips about 5mm/1/4in wide. Finely chop any tentacles. Set aside. Heat the oil in a frying pan, add the onion and cook gently, stirring, for about 5 minutes until softened. Add the squid, tomatoes, garlic, vinegar and sugar and stir to mix.

NUTRITIONAL NOTES
Per portion:

Energy	285Kcals/1206kJ
Total fat	4g
Saturated fat	0.4g
Cholesterol	0.0mg
Fibre	3g

2 Add the rosemary and seasoning. Bring to the boil, stirring, then cover, reduce the heat and simmer for 20 minutes, stirring occasionally. Stir in the peas and cook for a further 10 minutes. Cook the pasta according to the packet instructions. Serve with the sauce and the parsley.

HOT SPICY PRAWNS WITH CAMPANELLE

—

This low-fat prawn sauce tossed with hot pasta creates an ideal Italian-style supper dish. Add less or more chilli depending on how hot you like your food.

INGREDIENTS

225g/8oz cooked, peeled
tiger prawns (jumbo shrimp)
1–2 garlic cloves, crushed
finely grated rind of 1 lemon
15ml/1 tbsp fresh lemon juice
1.5ml/¼ tsp red chilli paste or 1 large
pinch of chilli powder
15ml/1 tbsp light soy sauce
150g/5oz lean smoked
bacon rashers (strips)
1 shallot or small onion,
finely chopped
60ml/4 tbsp dry white wine
225g/8oz/2 cups dried campanelle or
other dried pasta shapes
60ml/4 tbsp fish stock
4 firm ripe tomatoes, peeled,
seeded and chopped
30ml/2 tbsp chopped
fresh parsley
salt and freshly ground black pepper

SERVES 4

1 In a glass bowl, combine the prawns with the garlic, lemon rind and juice, then stir in the chilli paste or powder and light soy sauce.

2 Season with salt and pepper, then cover and leave to marinate in a cool place for at least 1 hour.

3 Grill (broil) the bacon rashers under a hot grill (broiler) until cooked, then cut them into 5mm/¼in dice. Set aside.

4 Put the shallot or onion and white wine into a pan, bring to the boil, cover and cook for 2–3 minutes or until it is tender and the wine has reduced by half. Remove from the heat and set aside.

5 Meanwhile, cook the pasta in a large pan of boiling salted water according to the packet instructions, until tender or *al dente*. Drain thoroughly and keep hot.

COOK'S TIP

To save time later, the prawns (shrimp) and marinade ingredients can be mixed together, covered and chilled in the refrigerator overnight.

6 Just before serving, put the prawns with their marinade into a large frying pan, bring to the boil quickly and add the cooked bacon and fish stock. Heat through for 1 minute, stirring.

7 Add to the hot pasta with the shallot or onion mixture, chopped tomatoes and parsley. Toss quickly to mix thoroughly and serve immediately.

NUTRITIONAL NOTES
Per portion:

Energy	214Kcals/908kJ
Total fat	3g
Saturated fat	0.9g
Cholesterol	37.5mg
Fibre	1.4g

SPAGHETTI WITH CLAM SAUCE

This is one of Italy's most famous pasta dishes, sometimes translated as "white clam sauce" to distinguish it from that other classic, clams in tomato sauce.

INGREDIENTS
1kg/2¼lb fresh clams
15ml/1 tbsp olive oil
45ml/3 tbsp chopped fresh flat leaf parsley
120ml/4fl oz/½ cup dry white wine
275g/10oz dried spaghetti
2 garlic cloves
salt and freshly ground black pepper

SERVES 4

1 Scrub the clams under cold running water, discarding any that are open or that do not close when sharply tapped against the work surface.

2 Heat half the oil in a large pan, add the clams and 15ml/1 tbsp of the parsley and cook over a high heat for a few seconds. Pour in the wine, then cover tightly. Cook for about 5 minutes, shaking the pan frequently, until the clams have opened. Meanwhile, cook the pasta in a large pan of boiling salted water, according to the packet instructions, until tender or *al dente*.

3 Using a slotted spoon, transfer the clams to a bowl, discarding any that have failed to open. Strain the liquid and set it aside. Put 8 clams to one side, then remove the rest from their shells.

4 Heat the remaining oil in a clean pan. Cook the whole garlic cloves over a medium heat until golden, crushing them with the back of a spoon. Remove the garlic with a slotted spoon and discard.

5 Add the shelled clams to the pan, gradually add some of the strained liquid from the clams, then add plenty of pepper. Cook for 1–2 minutes, gradually adding more liquid as the sauce reduces. Add the remaining parsley and cook for 1–2 minutes, stirring occasionally.

6 Drain the pasta, add it to the pan and toss well. Serve in individual dishes, scooping the shelled clams from the bottom of the pan and placing some of them on top of each serving. Garnish with the reserved clams in their shells and serve immediately.

NUTRITIONAL NOTES
Per portion:

Energy	425Kcals/1789kJ
Total fat	4.5g
Saturated fat	0.4g
Cholesterol	0mg
Fibre	1.5g

VERMICELLI WITH CLAM AND TOMATO SAUCE

—

This recipe originates from the city of Naples, where both fresh tomato sauce and seafood
are traditionally served with vermicelli. The two are combined for a tasty, low-fat dish.

INGREDIENTS

1kg/2¼lb fresh clams
250ml/8fl oz/1 cup dry white wine
2 garlic cloves, bruised
1 large handful of fresh flat leaf parsley
10ml/2 tsp olive oil
1 small onion, finely chopped
8 ripe Italian plum tomatoes, peeled,
seeded and finely chopped
½–1 fresh red chilli, seeded and
finely chopped
350g/12oz dried vermicelli
salt and freshly ground black pepper

SERVES 4

1 Scrub the clams thoroughly under cold
running water and discard any that are
open or that do not close when sharply
tapped against the work surface.

2 Pour the white wine into a large pan,
add the bruised garlic cloves and half the
parsley, then add the clams. Cover tightly
with a lid and bring to the boil over a
high heat. Cook for about 5 minutes,
shaking the pan frequently, until the
clams have opened.

3 Tip the clams into a large colander set
over a bowl and let the liquid drain
through. Leave the clams until cool
enough to handle, then remove about
two-thirds of them from their shells,
tipping the clam liquor into the bowl of
cooking liquid.

4 Discard any clams that have failed to
open. Set both shelled and unshelled
clams aside, keeping the unshelled clams
warm in a bowl covered with a lid.
Reserve the cooking liquid and set aside.

5 Heat the oil in a pan, add the onion and
cook gently, stirring frequently, for about
5 minutes until softened. Add the
tomatoes, then the clam liquid. Add the
chilli, season to taste and stir.

6 Bring to the boil, half cover, then
simmer gently for 15–20 minutes, stirring
occasionally. Meanwhile, cook the pasta
in a large pan of boiling salted water,
according to the packet instructions.
Chop the remaining parsley finely.

NUTRITIONAL NOTES
Per portion:

Energy	536Kcals/2262kJ
Total fat	4.7g
Saturated fat	0.4g
Cholesterol	0mg
Fibre	2.4g

7 Add the shelled clams to the sauce, stir
well and heat through very gently for
2–3 minutes, stirring occasionally.

8 Drain the cooked pasta well and tip it
into a warmed bowl. Taste the clam and
tomato sauce and adjust the seasoning,
then pour the sauce over the pasta and
toss everything together well. Garnish
with the reserved clams in their shells,
sprinkle the chopped parsley over the
pasta and serve immediately.

TRENETTE WITH SHELLFISH

Colourful and delicious, this typical pasta dish from the Genoese region of Italy is ideal for a low-fat lunch or supper. The sauce is quite runny, so serve it with spoons and crusty Italian bread.

INGREDIENTS

20ml/4 tsp olive oil
1 small onion, finely chopped
1 garlic clove, crushed
*1/2 fresh red chilli, seeded and
finely chopped*
*200g/7oz can chopped Italian
plum tomatoes*
30ml/2 tbsp chopped fresh flat leaf parsley
450g/1lb fresh clams in their shells
450g/1lb fresh mussels in their shells
60ml/4 tbsp dry white wine
450g/1lb/4 cups dried trenette
a few fresh basil leaves
*90g/3 1/2oz/2/3 cup cooked, peeled prawns
(shrimp) , thawed and dried if frozen*
salt and freshly ground black pepper
chopped fresh herbs, to garnish

SERVES 6

1 Heat half the oil in a frying pan. Add the onion, garlic and chilli and cook over a medium heat for 1–2 minutes, stirring constantly. Stir in the tomatoes, half the parsley and pepper to taste. Bring to the boil, cover, reduce the heat and simmer for 15 minutes, stirring occasionally.

2 Scrub the clams and mussels under cold running water. Discard any that are open or that do not close when sharply tapped against the work surface.

3 In a large pan, heat the remaining oil. Add the clams and mussels, with the rest of the parsley and toss over a high heat for a few seconds. Pour in the white wine, then cover tightly. Cook for about 5 minutes, shaking the pan frequently, until the clams and mussels have opened.

4 Remove the pan from the heat and transfer the clams and mussels to a bowl with a slotted spoon, discarding any shellfish that have failed to open.

NUTRITIONAL NOTES
Per portion:

Energy	414Kcals/1755kJ
Total fat	5g
Saturated fat	0.7g
Cholesterol	21mg
Fibre	2.7g

5 Strain the cooking liquid into a measuring jug (cup) and set aside. Reserve a few clams and mussels in their shells for the garnish, then remove the rest from their shells.

6 Cook the pasta in a large pan of boiling salted water, according to the packet instructions, until tender or *al dente*. Meanwhile, add 120ml/4fl oz/1/2 cup of the seafood liquid to the tomato sauce. Bring to the boil over a high heat, stirring. Reduce the heat, tear in the basil and add the prawns with the shelled clams and mussels. Stir well, then adjust the seasoning to taste.

7 Drain the pasta and tip it into a warmed bowl. Add the shellfish sauce and toss well to combine. Serve sprinkled with chopped herbs and garnish each portion with the reserved clams and mussels.

LINGUINE WITH CRAB

—

This pasta recipe comes from Rome. It makes a tasty low-fat first course served on its own, or it can be served for lunch or supper with crusty Italian bread.

INGREDIENTS
about 250g/9oz white crab meat
15ml/1 tbsp olive oil
1 small handful of fresh flat leaf parsley,
coarsely chopped, plus extra to garnish
1 garlic clove, crushed
350g/12oz ripe Italian plum tomatoes,
peeled and chopped
60–90ml/4–6 tbsp dry white wine
350g/12oz dried linguine
salt and freshly ground black pepper

SERVES 4

1 Put the crab meat in a mortar and pound to a rough pulp with a pestle, or use a sturdy bowl and the end of a rolling pin. Set aside.

2 Heat the oil in a large pan. Add the parsley and garlic, season to taste and cook until the garlic begins to brown, stirring occasionally.

NUTRITIONAL NOTES
Per portion:

Energy	308Kcals/1307kJ
Total fat	5g
Saturated fat	0.7g
Cholesterol	32.1mg
Fibre	2.3g

3 Stir in the tomatoes, pounded crab meat and wine, cover the pan, bring to the boil, then reduce the heat and simmer for 15 minutes, stirring occasionally.

4 Meanwhile, cook the pasta in a large pan of boiling salted water, according to the packet instructions, draining it the moment it is tender or *al dente*, and reserving a little of the cooking water. Return the pasta to the clean pan.

5 Add the tomato and crab mixture to the pasta and toss to mix, adding a little cooking water if necessary. Adjust the seasoning to taste. Serve hot, in warmed bowls, sprinkled with chopped parsley.

COOK'S TIP
Ask a fishmonger to remove crab meat from the shell, or buy dressed crab at the supermarket. Alternatively, use drained canned crab meat.

SEAFOOD AND SAFFRON PAPPARDELLE

—

Serve this flavourful and low-fat pasta dish with a mixed green salad and fresh Italian bread for a wholesome and nutritious meal.

INGREDIENTS

large pinch of saffron threads
4 sun-dried tomatoes, chopped
5ml/1 tsp chopped fresh thyme
12 large prawns (shrimp) in their shells
225g/8oz baby squid
225g/8oz skinless monkfish fillet
2–3 garlic cloves, crushed
2 small onions, quartered
1 small bulb fennel, trimmed and sliced
150ml/¼ pint/⅔ cup white wine
225g/8oz dried pappardelle
salt and freshly ground black pepper
30ml/2 tbsp chopped fresh parsley,
to garnish

SERVES 4

1 Put the saffron, sun-dried tomatoes and thyme into a bowl with 60ml/4 tbsp hot water. Leave to soak for 30 minutes.

COOK'S TIP

Make sure you use the sun-dried tomatoes for soaking in Step 1, rather than the ones preserved in oil. Do not try to substitute turmeric for the saffron in this recipe; although the colour will be similar, the flavour will be quite different.

2 Wash the prawns and carefully remove and discard the shells, but leave the heads and tails intact. Pull the head from the body of each squid and remove and discard the quill. Cut the tentacles from the head and rinse under cold water. Pull off and discard the outer skin and cut the flesh into 5mm/¼in rings. Cut the monkfish into 2.5cm/1in cubes. Set aside.

3 Put the garlic, onions and fennel into a pan with the wine. Cover and simmer for 5 minutes until tender. Stir occasionally.

NUTRITIONAL NOTES

Per portion:

Energy	381Kcals/1602kJ
Total fat	3.5g
Saturated fat	0.6g
Cholesterol	34mg
Fibre	3.2g

4 Stir in the monkfish and the saffron mixture. Cover and cook for 3 minutes, then stir in the prawns and squid. Cover and cook gently for 1–2 minutes (do not overcook). Season to taste.

5 Meanwhile, cook the pasta in a large pan of boiling, salted water according to the packet instructions, until tender or *al dente*. Drain thoroughly.

6 Divide the pasta among 4 serving dishes and top with the sauce. Sprinkle with parsley and serve immediately.

VEGETARIAN PASTA DISHES

This appetizing MEDLEY *of vegetarian pasta dishes brings together a wealth of* DELICIOUS *ingredients to create a collection of low-fat recipes* PACKED *with goodness and the flavours of Italy for family and friends to* RELISH. *Select from recipes such as Tagliatelle with Sun-Dried* TOMATOES, *Mushroom Bolognese, Penne with Artichokes or* TAGLIATELLE *with Hazelnut Pesto.*

CONCHIGLIE WITH TOMATOES AND ROCKET

—

Cooked pasta shells, tossed together with lightly cooked tomatoes and fresh rocket, makes a
tasty low-fat dish that is ideal for a summer lunch or supper.

INGREDIENTS

450g/1lb/4 cups dried conchiglie
450g/1lb ripe cherry tomatoes
75g/3oz fresh rocket (arugula)
15ml/1 tbsp extra virgin olive oil
15g/¹/₂oz fresh Parmesan cheese
salt and freshly ground black pepper

SERVES 4

1 Cook the pasta in a large pan of
boiling salted water, according to the
packet instructions, until tender or *al
dente*. Stir occasionally.

2 While the pasta is cooking, halve the
cherry tomatoes. Trim, wash and dry
the rocket.

3 Heat the oil in a large pan, add the
halved tomatoes and cook for barely
1 minute. The tomatoes should only just
heat through and not disintegrate.

4 Meanwhile, cut the Parmesan cheese
into fine shavings, using a swivel
vegetable peeler.

COOK'S TIP

This pasta dish relies for its success
on a salad green called rocket.
Available in most large supermarkets,
it is a leaf that is easily grown in the
garden or a window-box and tastes
slightly peppery. When you buy rocket,
make sure the leaves are very fresh
with no sign of wilting. Rocket does
not keep well unless it has been
pre-packaged. To keep it for a day or
two, wrap it in damp kitchen paper and
store in the refrigerator.

5 Drain the pasta and tip it into the pan
with the tomatoes.

6 Add the rocket and then carefully
stir to mix and heat through. Season
well with salt and pepper and serve
immediately, topped with a little shaved
Parmesan cheese.

VARIATIONS
• You might like to try adding
1.5ml/¹/₄ tsp dried chilli flakes and
2 finely chopped garlic cloves to
this dish. Simply add them to the oil
and fry gently for a minute or so
before adding the tomatoes.
• Use a different type of pasta, such
as fusilli, in place of the conchiglie.
• In place of the rocket, try
fresh watercress.

NUTRITIONAL NOTES
Per portion:

Energy	329Kcals/1396kJ
Total fat	5g
Saturated fat	1.2g
Cholesterol	2.3mg
Fibre	3.5g

TAGLIATELLE WITH SUN-DRIED TOMATOES

Tagliatelle tossed in a delicious fresh and sun-dried tomato sauce is an ideal main-course
meal for all the family to enjoy.

INGREDIENTS

1 garlic clove, crushed
1 celery stick, thinly sliced
115g/4oz/1 cup sun-dried tomatoes,
finely chopped
90ml/6 tbsp red wine
8 plum tomatoes
350g/12oz dried tagliatelle
salt and freshly ground black pepper

SERVES 4

1 Put the garlic, celery, sun-dried
tomatoes and wine into a pan. Cook gently
for 15 minutes, stirring occasionally.

2 Meanwhile, plunge the plum tomatoes
into a pan of boiling water for 1 minute,
then into a pan of cold water. Drain, then
slip off and discard their skins. Halve the
tomatoes, remove and discard the seeds
and cores and roughly chop the flesh.

3 Add the plum tomatoes to the pan of
vegetables, stir to mix and simmer for a
further 5 minutes. Season to taste with
salt and pepper.

NUTRITIONAL NOTES

Per portion:

Energy	357Kcals/1499kJ
Total fat	2.32g
Saturated fat	0.32g
Cholesterol	0mg
Fibre	5.09g

4 Meanwhile, cook the tagliatelle in a
large pan of boiling salted water for
8–10 minutes, until tender or *al dente*.
Drain well. Toss the cooked pasta with
half the tomato sauce and serve on
warmed plates, topped with the remaining
tomato sauce.

COOK'S TIP

Choose plain sun-dried tomatoes for
this sauce, instead of those preserved
in oil, which will increase the fat
content of the dish.

SPAGHETTI WITH MIXED BEAN SAUCE
—

Mixed beans are flavoured with fresh chilli and garlic and cooked in a tomato sauce
in this quick and easy pasta dish.

INGREDIENTS

1 onion, finely chopped
1–2 garlic cloves, crushed
1 large green chilli, seeded and
finely chopped
150ml/¼ pint/⅔ cup vegetable stock
400g/14oz can chopped tomatoes
30ml/2 tbsp tomato purée (paste)
120ml/4fl oz/½ cup red wine
5ml/1 tsp dried oregano
200g/7oz green beans, sliced
400g/14oz can red kidney beans, drained
400g/14oz can cannellini beans, drained
400g/14oz can chickpeas, drained
450g/1lb dried spaghetti
salt and freshly ground black pepper

SERVES 6

1 Put the onion, garlic and chilli into a
non-stick pan with the stock. Bring to the
boil and cook for 5 minutes until tender,
stirring occasionally.

NUTRITIONAL NOTES
Per portion:

Energy	431Kcals/1811kJ
Total fat	3.6g
Saturated fat	0.2g
Cholesterol	0mg
Fibre	9.9g

2 Stir in the tomatoes, tomato purée,
wine, oregano and seasoning. Bring to the
boil, cover, then reduce the heat and
simmer for 20 minutes, stirring the
mixture occasionally.

3 Meanwhile, cook the green beans in
a pan of boiling, salted water for about
5–6 minutes until tender. Drain the
beans thoroughly.

4 Add all the beans and the chickpeas to
the sauce, stir to mix and simmer for a
further 10 minutes. Meanwhile, cook the
spaghetti in a large pan of boiling salted
water, according to the packet
instructions, until tender or *al dente*.
Drain thoroughly. Transfer the pasta to a
serving dish and top with the bean sauce.
Serve immediately.

TAGLIATELLE WITH BROCCOLI AND SPINACH

This is an excellent vegetarian supper dish. It is nutritious, filling and low-fat and needs no
accompaniment. If you like, you can use tagliatelle flecked with herbs.

2 Add salt to the water in the steamer and
fill the steamer pan with boiling water,
then add the pasta and cook, according to
the packet instructions, until tender or *al
dente*. Meanwhile, chop the broccoli and
spinach in the colander.

INGREDIENTS
2 heads of broccoli
450g/1lb fresh spinach, stalks removed
freshly grated nutmeg
350g/12oz dried egg tagliatelle
15ml/1 tbsp extra virgin olive oil
juice of 1/2 lemon, or to taste
salt and freshly ground black pepper
*15g/1/2oz/2½ tbsp grated fresh Parmesan
cheese, to serve*

SERVES 4

NUTRITIONAL NOTES
Per portion:

Energy	288Kcals/1218kJ
Total fat	4.9g
Saturated fat	1g
Cholesterol	1.9mg
Fibre	4.5g

1 Put the broccoli in the basket of a
steamer, cover and steam over a pan of
boiling water for 10 minutes. Add the
spinach to the broccoli, cover and steam
for 4–5 minutes or until both are tender.
Towards the end of the cooking time,
sprinkle the vegetables with freshly
grated nutmeg and salt and pepper to
taste. Transfer the vegetables to a
colander and set aside.

3 Drain the pasta. Heat the oil in the
pasta pan, add the pasta and chopped
vegetables and toss over a medium heat
until evenly mixed. Sprinkle in the lemon
juice and plenty of black pepper, then
taste and add more lemon juice, salt and
nutmeg if you like. Serve immediately,
sprinkled with freshly grated Parmesan
and black pepper.

VARIATION
If you like, add a sprinkling of
crushed dried chillies with the black
pepper in Step 3.

PENNE WITH GREEN VEGETABLE SAUCE

Lightly cooked fresh green vegetables are tossed with pasta to create this low-fat dish, ideal for a light lunch or supper.

INGREDIENTS

2 carrots

1 courgette (zucchini)

75g/3oz green beans

1 small leek, washed

2 ripe Italian plum tomatoes

1 handful of fresh flat leaf parsley

15ml/1 tbsp extra virgin olive oil

2.5ml/¹/₂ tsp sugar

115g/4oz/1 cup frozen peas

350g/12oz/3 cups dried penne

salt and freshly ground black pepper

SERVES 4

1 Dice the carrots and the courgette finely. Trim the green beans, then cut them into 2cm/³/4in lengths. Slice the leek thinly. Peel and dice the tomatoes. Finely chop the parsley and set aside.

NUTRITIONAL NOTES

Per portion:

Energy	328Kcals/1392kJ
Total fat	4.5g
Saturated fat	0.7g
Cholesterol	0mg
Fibre	5g

2 Heat the oil in a medium frying pan. Add the carrots and leek. Sprinkle the sugar over and cook, stirring frequently, for about 5 minutes.

3 Stir in the courgette, green beans, peas and plenty of salt and pepper. Cover and cook over a low to medium heat for about 5–8 minutes until the vegetables are tender, stirring occasionally.

4 Meanwhile, cook the pasta in a large pan of boiling salted water, according to the packet instructions, until it is tender or *al dente*. Drain the pasta well, set aside and keep it hot until it is ready to serve.

5 Stir the parsley and chopped plum tomatoes into the vegetable mixture and adjust the seasoning to taste. Toss with the cooked pasta and serve immediately.

PAPPARDELLE AND SUMMER VEGETABLE SAUCE

A delicious low-fat sauce of tomatoes and fresh vegetables adds colour and robust flavour to pasta in this tasty Italian-style dish.

INGREDIENTS

2 small red onions, peeled, root left intact
150ml/1/4 pint/2/3 cup vegetable stock
1–2 garlic cloves, crushed
60ml/4 tbsp red wine
2 courgettes (zucchini), cut into fingers
1 yellow (bell) pepper, seeded and sliced
400g/14oz can tomatoes
10ml/2 tsp chopped fresh thyme
5ml/1 tsp caster (superfine) sugar
350g/12oz dried pappardelle
salt and freshly ground black pepper
fresh thyme and 6 black olives, pitted and coarsely chopped, to garnish

SERVES 4

1 Cut each onion into 8 wedges through the root end, to hold them together during cooking. Put into a pan with the stock and garlic. Bring to the boil, cover then reduce the heat and simmer gently for 5 minutes, until tender.

2 Add the wine, courgettes, yellow pepper, tomatoes, chopped thyme and sugar. Season with salt and pepper and stir to mix. Bring to the boil and cook gently for 5–7 minutes, shaking the pan occasionally to coat the vegetables with the sauce. (Do not overcook the vegetables as they are much nicer if they are slightly crunchy.)

3 Meanwhile, cook the pasta in a large pan of boiling salted water, according to the packet instructions, until tender or *al dente*. Drain thoroughly.

NUTRITIONAL NOTES
Per portion:

Energy	334Kcals/1426kJ
Total fat	2.1g
Saturated fat	0.3g
Cholesterol	0mg
Fibre	4g

4 Transfer the pasta to a warmed serving dish and top with the vegetables. Garnish with fresh thyme and chopped black olives and serve immediately.

PASTA PRIMAVERA
—

You can use any mixture of fresh, young spring vegetables to make this delicately flavoured
low-fat pasta dish, ideal for a quick and tasty supper.

INGREDIENTS

*225g/8oz thin asparagus spears, chopped
in half*
115g/4oz mangetouts (snow peas), trimmed
115g/4oz baby corn
225g/8oz whole baby carrots, trimmed
*1 small (bell) red pepper, seeded
and chopped*
8 spring onions (scallions), sliced
*225g/8oz dried torchietti or other
pasta shapes*
150g/5oz/2/3 cup low-fat cottage cheese
150ml/1/4 pint/2/3 cup low-fat yogurt
15ml/1 tbsp lemon juice
15ml/1 tbsp chopped fresh parsley
15ml/1 tbsp chopped fresh chives
skimmed milk (optional)
salt and freshly ground black pepper
sun-dried tomato bread, to serve

SERVES 4

3 Meanwhile, cook the pasta in a large
pan of boiling salted water, according to
the packet instructions, until tender or *al
dente*. Drain thoroughly and keep hot.

1 Cook the asparagus spears in a pan of
boiling, salted water for 3–4 minutes.
Add the mangetouts halfway through the
cooking time. Drain and rinse both under
cold water to stop further cooking, then
set aside.

2 Cook the baby corn, carrots, red pepper
and spring onions in the same way in a
pan of boiling salted water until tender.
Drain, rinse and set aside.

NUTRITIONAL NOTES
Per portion:

Energy	320Kcals/1344kJ
Total fat	3.1g
Saturated fat	0.4g
Cholesterol	3mg
Fibre	6.2g

4 Put the cottage cheese, yogurt, lemon
juice, parsley, chives and seasoning into a
blender or food processor and process
until smooth. Thin the sauce with a little
skimmed milk, if necessary. Put the sauce
into a large pan with the cooked pasta
and vegetables, heat gently and toss
carefully to mix. Serve at once with sun-
dried tomato bread.

LENTIL BOLOGNESE

Served with cooked spaghetti, this delicious lentil Bolognese sauce provides
an excellent low-fat pasta dish for all vegetarians.

INGREDIENTS

15ml/1 tbsp olive oil
1 onion, chopped
2 garlic cloves, crushed
2 carrots, coarsely grated
2 celery sticks, chopped
115g/4oz/½ cup red lentils
400g/14oz can chopped tomatoes
30ml/2 tbsp tomato purée (paste)
450ml/¾ pint/scant 2 cups stock
15ml/1 tbsp chopped fresh marjoram, or
5ml/1 tsp dried marjoram
450g/1lb dried spaghetti
salt and freshly ground black pepper

SERVES 6

1 Heat the oil in a large pan, add the
onion, garlic, carrots and celery and cook
gently for about 5 minutes, until the
vegetables are soft, stirring occasionally.

2 Add the lentils, tomatoes, tomato
purée, stock, marjoram and seasoning and
stir to mix.

3 Bring the mixture to the boil, then
partially cover with a lid, reduce the heat
and simmer for about 20 minutes until
thick and soft, stirring occasionally.

4 Meanwhile, cook the pasta in a
large pan of boiling salted water,
according to the packet instructions,
until tender or *al dente*. Drain well.

5 Serve the cooked pasta on warmed
serving plates, with the lentil sauce
spooned on top.

NUTRITIONAL NOTES
Per portion:

Energy	335Kcals/1423kJ
Total fat	3.4g
Saturated fat	0.4g
Cholesterol	3.9mg
Fibre	0g

TAGLIATELLE WITH HAZELNUT PESTO

Hazelnuts add a delicious flavour to this reduced-fat alternative to the classic Italian pesto sauce. Serve with cooked pasta, such as tagliatelle or fettuccine.

2 Cook the tagliatelle in a large pan of boiling salted water, according to the packet instructions, until tender or *al dente*, then drain well.

3 Add the pesto sauce to the hot pasta, tossing together until well mixed. Sprinkle with pepper and serve hot.

INGREDIENTS
2 garlic cloves, crushed
25g/1oz/1 cup fresh basil leaves
25g/1oz/¹/4 cup hazelnuts
200g/7oz/scant 1 cup skimmed milk soft cheese
225g/8oz dried tagliatelle, or 450g/1lb fresh
salt and freshly ground black pepper

SERVES 4

1 Place the garlic, basil, hazelnuts and soft cheese in a blender or food processor and process to a thick paste. Set aside.

NUTRITIONAL NOTES
Per portion:

Energy	227Kcals/960kJ
Total fat	4.7g
Saturated fat	0.7g
Cholesterol	2.1mg
Fibre	1.7g

PENNE WITH TOMATO AND CHILLI SAUCE

This is a speciality of Lazio. In Italian it is called *pasta all'arrabbiata* – the word *arrabbiata* means rabid or angry, and describes the heat that comes from the chilli.

INGREDIENTS

500g/1¼lb sugocasa
2 garlic cloves, crushed
150ml/¼ pint/⅔ cup dry white wine
15ml/1 tbsp sun-dried tomato purée (paste)
1 fresh red chilli
300g/11oz/2¾ cups dried penne
60ml/4 tbsp finely chopped fresh flat leaf parsley
salt and freshly ground black pepper
15g/½oz/2½ tbsp grated fresh Pecorino cheese, to serve

SERVES 4

3 Remove the chilli from the sauce and add half the parsley. Add seasoning to taste. If you prefer a hotter taste, finely chop some or all of the chilli and return it to the sauce.

4 Drain the pasta and tip it into a warmed serving bowl. Pour the sauce over the pasta and toss to mix. Serve immediately, sprinkled with a little grated Pecorino cheese and the remaining parsley.

NUTRITIONAL NOTES
Per portion:

Energy	287Kcals/1220kJ
Total fat	2.1g
Saturated fat	0.7g
Cholesterol	2.2mg
Fibre	3g

1 Put the sugocasa, garlic, wine, tomato purée and whole chilli in a pan and bring to the boil. Cover, reduce the heat and simmer gently, stirring occasionally.

2 Drop the pasta into a large pan of rapidly boiling salted water and simmer for 10–12 minutes, until tender or *al dente*.

PENNE WITH ARTICHOKES

—

Artichokes are a very popular vegetable in Italy, and are often used in sauces for pasta. This sauce is garlicky and richly flavoured, perfect for a delicious light lunch or supper.

INGREDIENTS

juice of 1/2–1 lemon
2 globe artichokes
15ml/1 tbsp olive oil
1 small fennel bulb, thinly sliced, with feathery tops reserved
1 onion, finely chopped
4 garlic cloves, finely chopped
1 handful of fresh flat leaf parsley, coarsely chopped
400g/14oz can chopped Italian plum tomatoes
150ml/1/4 pint/2/3 cup dry white wine
350g/12oz/3 cups dried penne
10ml/2 tsp capers, chopped
salt and freshly ground black pepper

SERVES 6

1 Have ready a bowl of cold water to which you have added the juice of half a lemon. Cut off the artichoke stalks, then discard the outer leaves until only the pale inner leaves that are almost white at the base remain.

2 Cut off the tops of these leaves so that the base remains. Cut the base in half lengthways, then prise the hairy choke out of the centre with the tip of the knife and discard. Cut the artichokes lengthways into 5mm/1/4in slices, adding them immediately to the bowl of water.

3 Bring a large pan of water to the boil. Add a good pinch of salt, then drain the artichokes and add them immediately to the water. Boil for 5 minutes, drain and set aside.

4 Heat the olive oil in a large frying pan and add the fennel, onion, garlic and flat leaf parsley. Cook over a low to medium heat, stirring frequently, for about 10 minutes until the fennel has softened and is lightly coloured.

5 Add the tomatoes and wine and season with salt and pepper to taste. Bring to the boil, stirring, then cover, reduce the heat and simmer for 10–15 minutes, stirring occasionally. Stir in the artichokes, replace the lid and simmer for a further 10 minutes.

6 Meanwhile, cook the pasta in a large pan of water, according to the packet instructions. Drain, reserving a little cooking water. Stir the capers into the sauce, then adjust the seasoning and add the remaining lemon juice if you like.

7 Tip the pasta into a warmed serving bowl, pour the sauce over and mix, adding a little cooking water if necessary. Serve, garnished with fennel fronds.

NUTRITIONAL NOTES
Per portion:

Energy	269Kcals/1140kJ
Total fat	3g
Saturated fat	0.4g
Cholesterol	0mg
Fibre	2.7g

CHIFFERI RIGATI WITH AUBERGINE SAUCE

Full of flavour, this excellent vegetarian sauce goes well with any short pasta shape, such as chifferi rigati or penne, to create an appetizing lunch or supper dish.

2 Remove and discard the chilli. Add the aubergines to the pan with the remaining parsley and all the basil. Pour in half the water. Crumble in the stock cube and stir until it is dissolved, then cover and cook, stirring frequently, for about 10 minutes.

3 Add the tomatoes, wine, sugar, saffron and paprika, with salt and pepper to taste, then pour in the remaining water. Stir well, replace the lid and cook for a further 30–40 minutes, stirring occasionally. Adjust the seasoning to taste.

4 Meanwhile, cook the pasta in a large pan of boiling salted water, according to the packet instructions, until tender or *al dente*. Drain well.

5 Add the aubergine sauce to the cooked pasta, toss together to ensure they are thoroughly mixed and serve immediately.

INGREDIENTS
30ml/2 tbsp olive oil
1 small fresh red chilli
2 garlic cloves
2 handfuls of fresh flat leaf parsley
450g/1lb aubergines (eggplants),
coarsely chopped
1 handful of fresh basil leaves
200ml/7fl oz/scant 1 cup water
1 vegetable stock (bouillon) cube
8 ripe Italian plum tomatoes, peeled and
finely chopped
60ml/4 tbsp red wine
5ml/1 tsp sugar
1 sachet saffron powder
2.5ml/¹/₂ tsp ground paprika
450g/1lb/4 cups dried chifferi rigati
salt and freshly ground black pepper

SERVES 6

1 Heat the oil in a large frying pan and add the whole chilli and whole garlic cloves. Coarsely chop the parsley and add half of it to the pan. Smash the garlic cloves with a wooden spoon to release their juice, then cover the pan and cook the mixture over a low to medium heat for about 10 minutes, stirring occasionally.

NUTRITIONAL NOTES
Per portion:

Energy	300Kcals/1274kJ
Total fat	3.6g
Saturated fat	0.6g
Cholesterol	0mg
Fibre	4.1g

RIGATONI WITH WINTER TOMATO SAUCE

In winter, when fresh tomatoes are not at their best, this is the sauce the Italians make.
Try to use good-quality canned plum tomatoes from Italy.

INGREDIENTS

1 onion
1 carrot
1 celery stick
15ml/1 tbsp olive oil
1 garlic clove, thinly sliced
a few leaves each of fresh basil, thyme and oregano or marjoram, plus extra to garnish (optional)
2 × 400g/14oz cans chopped Italian plum tomatoes
15ml/1 tbsp sun-dried tomato purée (paste)
5ml/1 tsp sugar
about 90ml/6 tbsp dry red or white wine (optional)
350g/12oz/3 cups dried rigatoni
salt and freshly ground black pepper
15g/¹/₂oz coarsely shaved fresh Parmesan cheese, to serve (optional)

SERVES 4

1 Chop the onion, carrot and celery finely, either in a food processor or by hand.

2 Heat the oil in a medium pan, add the garlic slices and stir over a very low heat for 1–2 minutes.

3 Add the onion, carrot, celery and the fresh herbs. Cook over a low heat, stirring frequently, for 5–7 minutes until the vegetables have softened and have become lightly coloured.

4 Add the canned tomatoes, tomato purée and sugar, then stir in the wine, if using. Add salt and pepper to taste. Bring to the boil, stirring, then reduce the heat to a gentle simmer. Cook, uncovered, for about 45 minutes, stirring occasionally.

5 Meanwhile, cook the pasta in a large pan of boiling salted water, according to the packet instructions, until tender or *al dente*. Drain the pasta and tip it into a warmed bowl. Taste the sauce and adjust the seasoning. Pour the sauce over the pasta and toss well to mix. Serve immediately, with shavings of Parmesan handed separately, if using. If you like, garnish with extra chopped fresh herbs.

NUTRITIONAL NOTES
Per portion:

Energy	351Kcals/1491kJ
Total fat	4.4g
Saturated fat	0.6g
Cholesterol	0mg
Fibre	4g

FUSILLI WITH TOMATO AND BALSAMIC VINEGAR

The intense, sweet-and-sour flavour of balsamic vinegar gives a pleasant kick to this sauce made
with canned tomatoes. It makes an appetizing low-fat pasta meal.

INGREDIENTS

2 × 400g/14oz cans chopped Italian
plum tomatoes
2 pieces of drained sun-dried tomatoes in
olive oil, thinly sliced
2 garlic cloves, crushed
15ml/1 tbsp olive oil
5ml/1 tsp sugar
350g/12oz/3 cups dried fusilli
45ml/3 tbsp balsamic vinegar
salt and freshly ground black pepper
15g/¹/₂oz coarsely shaved
fresh Pecorino cheese and rocket (arugula)
salad, to serve (optional)

SERVES 4

1 Put the canned and sun-dried tomatoes
in a medium pan with the garlic, olive
oil and sugar. Season with salt and pepper
to taste. Bring to the boil, stirring
constantly. Reduce the heat and simmer,
stirring the mixture occasionally, for
about 30 minutes until reduced.

2 Meanwhile, cook the pasta in a
large saucepan of boiling salted water,
according to the packet instructions,
until tender or *al dente*.

3 Add the balsamic vinegar to the tomato
sauce and stir to mix evenly. Cook for
1–2 minutes then remove from the heat
and adjust the seasoning to taste.

4 Drain the pasta and turn it into a
warmed bowl. Pour the sauce over the
cooked pasta and toss well to mix. Serve
immediately, with the rocket salad and
shaved Pecorino handed around
separately, if using.

VARIATION
The flavour of carrots goes well with
balsamic vinegar. Try adding some fine
batons to the pan with the tomatoes
and garlic in Step 1.

NUTRITIONAL NOTES
Per portion:

Energy	360Kcals/1531kJ
Total fat	4.5g
Saturated fat	0.6g
Cholesterol	0mg
Fibre	4.1g

SPAGHETTI WITH FRESH TOMATO SAUCE

—

This is the famous Neapolitan sauce from Italy that is made in summer when tomatoes are very ripe and sweet. Spaghetti is the traditional choice of pasta for a low-fat, flavourful Italian meal.

INGREDIENTS

675g/1¹/2lb ripe Italian plum tomatoes
15ml/1 tbsp olive oil
1 onion, finely chopped
350g/12oz dried spaghetti
1 small handful of fresh basil leaves
salt and freshly ground black pepper
15g/¹/2oz coarsely shaved fresh Parmesan cheese, to serve

SERVES 4

1 With a sharp knife, cut a cross in the bottom (flower) end of each tomato. Bring a medium pan of water to the boil and remove from the heat. Plunge a few of the tomatoes into the water, leave for about 30 seconds, then lift them out with a slotted spoon. Repeat the process with the remaining tomatoes, then peel off and discard the skins and roughly chop the flesh. Set aside.

NUTRITIONAL NOTES
Per portion:

Energy	330Kcals/1399kJ
Total fat	5g
Saturated fat	1.1g
Cholesterol	2.2mg
Fibre	4.05g

2 Heat the oil in a large pan, add the onion and cook over a low heat, stirring frequently, for about 5 minutes until softened and lightly coloured. Add the tomatoes, with salt and pepper to taste. Bring to a gentle boil, then cover the pan, reduce the heat and simmer for about 30–40 minutes, stirring occasionally, until thick.

3 Meanwhile, cook the pasta in a large pan of boiling salted water, according to the packet instructions, until tender or *al dente*. Shred the fresh basil leaves finely.

4 Remove the sauce from the heat, stir in the basil and adjust the seasoning to taste. Drain the pasta, tip it into a warmed bowl, pour the sauce over and toss well to mix. Serve immediately, with a little shaved Parmesan handed separately.

PASTA WITH CHICKPEA SAUCE

—

This is a delicious, and very speedy, low-fat dish,
ideal for an appetizing lunch or supper.

INGREDIENTS

450g/1lb/4 cups dried penne or other dried
pasta shapes
10ml/2 tsp olive oil
1 onion, thinly sliced
1 red (bell) pepper, seeded and sliced
400g/14oz can chopped tomatoes
425g/15oz can chickpeas
30ml/2 tbsp dry vermouth (optional)
5ml/1 tsp dried oregano
1 large bay leaf
30ml/2 tbsp capers
salt and freshly ground black pepper
fresh oregano sprigs, to garnish

SERVES 6

1 Cook the pasta in a large pan of boiling
salted water, according to the packet
instructions, until tender or *al dente*.
Drain and keep hot. Meanwhile, heat the
olive oil in a large pan, add the sliced
onion and pepper and cook gently for
about 5 minutes, stirring occasionally,
until softened.

2 Add the tomatoes, chickpeas with their
liquid, vermouth, if using, herbs and
capers and stir well to mix.

3 Season to taste with salt and pepper
and bring to the boil, then reduce the heat
and simmer for about 10 minutes, stirring
occasionally. Remove and discard the bay
leaf. Add the hot pasta to the sauce, toss
to mix and serve hot, garnished with fresh
oregano sprigs.

COOK'S TIP

Choose whatever pasta shapes you like,
although hollow shapes, such as penne
(quills) or shells, are particularly good
with this sauce.

NUTRITIONAL NOTES

Per portion:

Energy	372Kcals/1579kJ
Total fat	4.9g
Saturated fat	0.6g
Cholesterol	0mg
Fibre	6g

TAGLIATELLE WITH MUSHROOMS

Freshly cooked tagliatelle is tossed with a flavourful mixed mushroom sauce, to create this very tasty, low-fat pasta dish.

3 Remove the lid from the pan and boil until the liquid has reduced by half, stirring occasionally. Stir in the chopped fresh herbs and season to taste with salt and pepper.

4 Meanwhile, cook the fresh pasta in a large pan of boiling, salted water for 2–5 minutes, until tender or *al dente*. Drain thoroughly, then toss the pasta lightly with the mushroom sauce. Serve, garnished with parsley and shavings of Parmesan cheese, if you like.

INGREDIENTS

1 small onion, finely chopped
2 garlic cloves, crushed
150ml/¼ pint/⅔ cup vegetable stock
225g/8oz mixed fresh mushrooms, such as field (portabello), chestnut or oyster
60ml/4 tbsp white or red wine
10ml/2 tsp tomato purée (paste)
15ml/1 tbsp soy sauce
5ml/1 tsp chopped fresh thyme
30ml/2 tbsp chopped fresh parsley, plus extra to garnish
225g/8oz fresh sun-dried tomato and herb tagliatelle
salt and freshly ground black pepper
15g/½oz shaved fresh Parmesan cheese, to serve (optional)

SERVES 4

1 Put the onion and garlic into a pan with the vegetable stock, then cover and cook for 5 minutes or until tender, stirring occasionally.

2 Add the mushrooms (quartered or sliced if large; left whole if small), wine, tomato purée and soy sauce. Cover and cook for 5 minutes, stirring occasionally.

NUTRITIONAL NOTES
Per portion:

Energy	241Kcals/1010kJ
Total fat	2.4g
Saturated fat	0.7g
Cholesterol	45mg
Fibre	3g

MUSHROOM BOLOGNESE

A quick – and exceedingly tasty – vegetarian version of the classic Italian dish. This dish is easy
to prepare and makes a very satisfying low-fat meal.

INGREDIENTS

450g/1lb mushrooms
15ml/1 tbsp olive oil
1 onion, chopped
1 garlic clove, crushed
15ml/1 tbsp tomato purée (paste)
400g/14oz can chopped tomatoes
45ml/3 tbsp chopped fresh oregano
*450g/1lb fresh pasta, such as spaghetti
or tagliatelle*
salt and freshly ground black pepper
*15g/¹/₂oz shaved fresh Parmesan cheese,
to serve (optional)*

SERVES 4

3 Add the prepared mushrooms to the
pan and mix them gently with the olive
oil and crushed garlic. Cook over a high
heat for about 3–4 minutes, stirring the
mixture occasionally.

5 Meanwhile, bring a large pan of salted
water to the boil. Cook the pasta in the
boiling water for about 2–3 minutes, or
according to the packet instructions, until
tender or *al dente*.

1 Trim the mushroom stems neatly, then
cut each mushroom into quarters. Set
them aside.

2 Heat the olive oil in a large pan. Add
the onion and garlic and cook them for
2–3 minutes, stirring occasionally.

4 Stir in the tomato purée, chopped
tomatoes and 15ml/1 tbsp of the oregano.
Cover, reduce the heat, then cook for
about 5 minutes, stirring occasionally.

COOK'S TIP
If you prefer to use dried pasta, make
this the first thing that you cook. It will
take 10–12 minutes to cook, during
which time you can make the
mushroom mixture. Use 350g/12oz
dried pasta.

6 Season the mushroom Bolognese sauce
with salt and pepper. Drain the pasta,
turn it into a bowl and add the mushroom
mixture. Toss to mix well. Serve in
individual bowls, topped with shavings
of fresh Parmesan, if using, and the
remaining chopped fresh oregano.

NUTRITIONAL NOTES
Per portion:

Energy	404Kcals/1717kJ
Total fat	4.9g
Saturated fat	0.6g
Cholesterol	0mg
Fibre	5g

TAGLIATELLE WITH SPINACH GNOCCHI

—

Italian-style gnocchi are extremely smooth and light and make a delicious accompaniment to this flavourful low-fat pasta dish.

INGREDIENTS
*450g/1lb mixed flavoured
fresh tagliatelle
15g/¹/₂oz shaved fresh Parmesan cheese,
to garnish (optional)*

FOR THE SPINACH GNOCCHI
*450g/1lb frozen chopped spinach
1 small onion, finely chopped
1 garlic clove, crushed
1.5ml/¹/₄ tsp ground nutmeg
400g/14oz/1¾ cups low-fat cottage cheese
115g/4oz/1⅔ cups dried
white breadcrumbs
75g/3oz/¹/₂ cup semolina
50g/2oz/⅔ cup grated Parmesan cheese
3 egg whites*

FOR THE TOMATO SAUCE
*1 onion, finely chopped
1 celery stick, finely chopped
1 red (bell) pepper, seeded and diced
1 garlic clove, crushed
150ml/¹/₄ pint/²/₃ cup vegetable stock
400g/14oz can tomatoes
15ml/1 tbsp tomato purée (paste)
10ml/2 tsp caster (superfine) sugar
5ml/1 tsp dried oregano
salt and freshly ground black pepper*

SERVES 6

1 To make the tomato sauce, put the onion, celery, pepper and garlic into a pan. Add the stock, bring to the boil and cook for 5 minutes, stirring occasionally.

2 Stir in the tomatoes, tomato purée, sugar and oregano. Season to taste, bring to the boil, then reduce the heat and simmer for 30 minutes until thick, stirring occasionally. Keep hot.

3 Meanwhile, make the gnocchi. Put the spinach, onion and garlic into a medium pan, cover and cook until the spinach is just thawed. Remove the lid for a minute or so, and increase the heat. Cook until all the liquid has evaporated. Season to taste with salt, pepper and nutmeg. Turn into a bowl and leave to cool. Mix in the remaining gnocchi ingredients. Shape into about 30 ovals and chill in the refrigerator for 30 minutes.

4 Cook the spinach gnocchi in a large pan of boiling salted water for about 5 minutes. Remove with a slotted spoon and drain. Keep hot. Meanwhile, cook the tagliatelle in a large pan of boiling salted water, according to the packet instructions, until tender or *al dente*. Drain well. Transfer the pasta to serving plates, top with the gnocchi, the tomato sauce and shavings of Parmesan cheese, if using. Serve immediately.

NUTRITIONAL NOTES
Per portion:

Energy	189Kcals/803kJ
Total fat	2g
Saturated fat	0.8g
Cholesterol	3.3mg
Fibre	2.9g

RATATOUILLE PENNE BAKE

Mixed Mediterranean vegetables and penne are tossed together and cooked until lightly
toasted to create this delicious and low-fat pasta meal.

3 Put the aubergine, courgettes, red
pepper, onion and remaining garlic into
a pan, with the stock. Bring to the boil,
cover and cook for about 10 minutes until
tender, stirring occasionally. Remove
the lid and boil until all the stock has
evaporated. Add the prepared tomatoes
and herbs and cook for a further
3 minutes, stirring occasionally. Season
to taste with salt and pepper.

INGREDIENTS

1 small aubergine (eggplant)
2 courgettes (zucchini), thickly sliced
200g/7oz firm beancurd (tofu), cubed
45ml/3 tbsp dark soy sauce
2–3 garlic cloves, crushed
10ml/2 tsp sesame seeds
1 small red (bell) pepper, seeded and sliced
1 onion, finely chopped
150ml/¼ pint/⅔ cup vegetable stock
3 firm ripe tomatoes, peeled, seeded
and quartered
15ml/1 tbsp chopped fresh mixed herbs
225g/8oz/2 cups dried penne
salt and freshly ground black pepper
crusty bread, to serve

SERVES 6

1 Wash and cut the aubergine into
2.5cm/1in cubes. Put into a colander with
the courgettes, sprinkle with salt and
leave to drain for 30 minutes. Rinse
thoroughly, drain and set aside.

2 Mix the beancurd with the soy sauce,
1 crushed garlic clove and the sesame
seeds. Cover and leave to marinate for
30 minutes.

NUTRITIONAL NOTES
Per portion:

Energy	208Kcals/873kJ
Total fat	3.7g
Saturated fat	0.5g
Cholesterol	0mg
Fibre	3.9g

4 Meanwhile cook the pasta in a large
pan of boiling salted water, according to
the packet instructions, until tender or *al
dente*. Drain thoroughly. Toss the pasta
with the vegetable mixture, the beancurd
and the marinade. Transfer to a shallow
25cm/10in square ovenproof dish and
cook under a hot grill (broiler) until
lightly toasted. Transfer the bake to a
serving dish and serve immediately with
fresh crusty bread.

INDEX

Agnolotti, consommé with, 28
Artichokes, penne with, 85
Aubergine sauce, chifferi rigati with, 86

Bacon, 6
Balsamic vinegar, fusilli with tomato and, 88
Beans, 8, 10
  spaghetti with mixed bean sauce, 77
Beef:
  chilli mince and pipe rigate, 39
  lasagne, 42
  spaghetti with meatballs, 40
  spaghetti with spicy beef sauce, 41
  tagliatelle with meat sauce, 44
Broccoli:
  macaroni with broccoli and cauliflower, 57
  tagliatelle with broccoli and spinach, 78
Broth:
  little stuffed hats in, 22
  tiny pasta in, 22
Buying pasta, 12

Calories, 7
Campanelle with hot spicy prawns, 64
Cannelloni with smoked trout, 58
Carbohydrates, 7, 9
Cauliflower, macaroni with broccoli and, 57
Cheese, 7, 9, 10
Chicken, 10, 11
  chicken and pasta soup, 25
  spicy chicken salad, 32
Chickpeas:
  pasta and chickpea soup, 24
  pasta with chickpea sauce, 90
Chifferi rigati with aubergine sauce, 86
Chillies:
  chilli and pipe rigate, 39
  penne with tomato and chilli sauce, 84
Cholesterol, 9
Clams:
  clam and pasta soup, 27
  spaghetti with clam sauce, 66
  vermicelli with clam and tomato sauce, 67
Conchiglie with tomatoes and rocket, 74
Consommé with agnolotti, 28
Crab:
  crab pasta salad with spicy dressing, 31
  linguine with crab, 69

Dairy products, 8, 9
Duck and pasta salad, 34

Farfalle:
  farfalle salad with piquant peppers, 30
  farfalle with tuna, 56
Fats, 6–7, 8–9
  cutting down on, 10
Fish, 8, 9, 11
  also see trout, tuna etc
Food groups, 8
Fusilli with smoked trout, 60

Fusilli with tomato and balsamic vinegar, 88

Garlic, 7
Gnocchi, 13
  tagliatelle with spinach gnocchi, 94

Ham, tagliolini with meaty tomato sauce, 46
Healthy eating guidelines, 6, 8–9
Herbs, 11
  pasta with herbed scallops, 61
Hidden fats, 9
Hot spicy prawns with campanelle, 64

Lamb and sweet pepper sauce, 45
Lasagne, 16, 42
Lentils, 8, 10
  lentil Bolognese, 82
Linguine with crab, 69
Little stuffed hats in broth, 22

Macaroni with broccoli and cauliflower, 57
Meat, 7, 8, 10, 11
Milk, 8, 9, 10
Minestrone:
  Puglia-style minestrone, 20
  vegetable minestrone, 21
Monounsaturated fats, 9
Mozzarella, 6
Mushrooms:
  mushroom Bolognese, 92
  tagliatelle with mushrooms, 91

Nuts, 7, 9
  tagliatelle with hazelnut pesto, 83

Oils, 9, 10, 11
Olive oil, 6, 7
Olives, 7

Pappardelle:
  pappardelle and summer vegetable sauce, 80
  pappardelle with rabbit sauce, 51
  seafood and saffron pappardelle, 70
Parmesan, 6
Pasta, 7, 8, 9, 10, 12–13, 14–17
Peas, 8, 10, 11
  spaghetti with squid and peas, 62
Penne:
  penne with artichokes, 85
  penne with green vegetable sauce, 79
  penne with tomato and chilli sauce, 84

Peppers:
  farfalle salad with piquant peppers, 30
  lamb and sweet pepper sauce, 45
Pesto, tagliatelle with hazelnut, 83
Pipe rigate and chilli mince, 39
Polyunsaturated fats, 9
Pork:
  rigatoni with pork, 47
  spaghetti alla carbonara, 50
  tagliatelle with meat sauce, 44
Poultry, 8, 11
Prawns, hot spicy prawns with campanelle, 64
Puglia-style minestrone, 20

Rabbit sauce, pappardelle with, 51
Ratatouille penne bake, 95
Ravioli, 16
Rigate and chilli mince, 39
Rigatoni:
  rigatoni with pork, 47
  rigatoni with winter tomato sauce, 87
Roasted tomato and pasta soup, 26
Rocket, conchiglie with tomatoes and, 74

Salads:
  crab pasta salad with spicy dressing, 31
  duck and pasta salad, 34
  farfalle salad with piquant peppers, 30
  spicy chicken salad, 32
Salami, 6
Saturated fats, 9
Scallops:
  black tagliatelle with creamy scallops, 61
  tagliatelle with scallops, 62
Seafood:
  and saffron pappardelle, 70
  see also clams, prawns etc
Smoked trout with cannelloni, 58
Smoked trout with fusilli, 60
Soups:
  chicken and pasta soup, 25
  clam and pasta soup, 27
  consommé with agnolotti, 28
  little stuffed hats in broth, 22
  pasta and chickpea soup, 24
  Puglia-style minestrone, 20
  roasted tomato and pasta soup, 26
  tiny pasta in broth, 22
  vegetable minestrone, 21
Spaghetti, 16
  spaghetti alla carbonara, 50
  spaghetti Bolognese, 38
  spaghetti with clam sauce, 66
  spaghetti with fresh tomato sauce, 89
  spaghetti with meatballs, 40
  spaghetti with mixed bean sauce, 77
  spaghetti with spicy beef sauce, 41
  spaghetti with squid and peas, 62
  spaghetti with tuna sauce, 54
Spices, 11,
Spinach:
  tagliatelle with broccoli and spinach, 78

  tagliatelle with spinach gnocchi, 94
Squid and peas with spaghetti, 64

Tagliatelle, 16, 17
  black tagliatelle with creamy scallops, 62
  tagliatelle with broccoli and spinach, 78
  tagliatelle with hazelnut pesto, 83
  tagliatelle with meat sauce, 44
  tagliatelle with Milanese sauce, 48
  tagliatelle with mushrooms, 91
  tagliatelle with spinach gnocchi, 94
  tagliatelle with sun-dried tomatoes, 76
Tagliolini with meaty tomato sauce, 46
Tiny pasta in broth, 22
Tomatoes:
  conchiglie with tomatoes and rocket, 74
  fusilli with tomato and balsamic vinegar, 88
  pasta with tomato and tuna, 55
  penne with tomato and chilli sauce, 84
  rigatoni with winter tomato sauce, 87
  roasted tomato and pasta soup, 26
  spaghetti with fresh tomato sauce, 89
  tagliatelle with sun-dried tomatoes, 76
  tagliolini with meaty tomato sauce, 46
  vermicelli with clam and tomato sauce,
Trenette with shellfish, 68
Trout:
  trout, smoked, with cannelloni, 58
  trout, smoked, with fusilli, 60
Tuna:
  tuna, pasta with tomato and, 55
  tuna sauce with spaghetti, 54
  tuna with farfalle, 56
Turkey:
  chilli mince and pipe rigate, 39
  lasagne, 42

Vegetables, 7, 8, 10, 11
  pappardelle and summer vegetable sauce, 80
  pasta primavera, 81
  penne with green vegetable sauce, 79
  vegetable minestrone, 21
Vermicelli with clam and tomato sauce, 67